D0056456

★ ★ ★ ★

Hollywood Babble On

★ ★ ★ ★

U.S. titles by the same author:

THE FILMS OF JANE FONDA
(Citadel Press)

CONVERSATIONS WITH MY ELDERS

HISPANIC HOLLYWOOD
(Citadel Press)

THE VINYL CLOSET

THE LAVENDER SCREEN
(Citadel Press)

☆ ☆ ☆ ☆

Hollywood Babble On

☆ ☆ ☆ ☆

Stars Gossip About
Other Stars

Boze Hadleigh

A Birch Lane Press Book
Published by Carol Publishing Group

For Ronnie

Copyright © 1994 by Boze Hadleigh
All rights reserved. No part of this book may be reproduced in any form,
except by a newspaper or magazine reviewer who wishes to quote brief
passages in connection with a review.

A Birch Lane Press Book
Published by Carol Publishing Group
Birch Lane Press is a registered trademark of Carol Communications, Inc.
Editorial Offices: 600 Madison Avenue, New York, N.Y. 10022
Sales and Distribution Offices: 120 Enterprise Avenue, Secaucus, N.J. 07094
In Canada: Canadian Manda Group, P.O. Box 920, Station U, Toronto, Ontario
    M8Z 5P9
Queries regarding rights and permissions should be addressed to Carol
Publishing Group, 600 Madison Avenue, New York, N.Y. 10022

Carol Publishing Group books are available at special discounts for bulk
purchases, for sales promotions, fund-raising, or educational purposes.
Special editions can be created to specifications. For details, contact Special
Sales Department, Carol Publishing Group, 120 Enterprise Avenue, Secaucus,
N.J. 07094

Manufactured in the United States of America
10 9 8 7 6 5 4 3 2 1

Library of Congress Cataloging-in-Publication Data

Hadleigh, Boze.
    Hollywood babble on : stars gossip about other stars / Boze Hadleigh.
       p. cm.
    "A Birch Lane Press book."
    ISBN 1-55972-219-3
    1. Motion picture actors and actresses—United States—Quotations.
    2. Motion picture industry—Anecdotes. I. Title.
PN1994.9.H25 1994
791.43'028'0922—dc20
                                                                    93-44644
                                                                    CIP

Contents

☆ ☆ ☆ ☆

Hollywood has to be seen to be disbelieved.
—Walter Winchell

Half the people in Hollywood are dying to be discovered. The other half are afraid they will be.
—Lionel Barrymore

Underneath all the phony tinsel of Hollywood...lies the real tinsel.
—Oscar Levant

Hollywood is a place where you spend more than you make, on things you don't need, to impress people you don't like.
—Ken Murray

☆ ☆ ☆ ☆

Preface

Most everyone has at one time or another gossiped about the stars. Not so much about the entertainment they bring us but about the individuals behind the celluloid façades. With more and more leisure time and with celebrity journalism and biography more prominent than ever, we find the stars looming larger and closer in our conversations and speculation.

Of course, the word "gossip" by now has a negative connotation and is incorrectly used to describe factual tidbits or wider information about a star's offscreen life. Gossip and rumor are not the same thing. However, because Tinseltown specializes in fake reality, the *real* tinsel is far more rare than the standardized, image-conscious, phony tinsel that studios, publicists, and the stars themselves continue to feed a not so gullible public.

Star gossip is intrinsically fascinating. But how much more insightful—and stinging!—is gossip about stars by *other* stars. By celebrities who are in the know and who, in an unguarded or indiscreet moment, may shed new light on a famous colleague whom we thought we knew so well.

Because the stars are as human as anyone, their revelations may be motivated by envy, cynicism, or spite. But star quotes, already newsworthy by nature, are far more interesting when focused on—or aimed at—another star. A clash of the titans, so to speak.

All of the quotes in this collection were uttered in print or on TV, in newspapers, magazines, interviews, memoirs, biographies—and biomythographies!—or in foreign periodicals and publications. For convenience and unity of theme, the collection is divided into eight chapters:

In the Slimelight—negative dish on stars in general.

Meow!—women being catty about other women. (Yes, men can be just as catty, but bear with me.)

All About Divas—women, but mostly men, tattling about female icons.

Ex-Husbands and -Wives—male-female couples—not all contractually married, some widowed—spotlighting their bitter half.

Lavender Limelight—dish on gay, lesbian, or bisexual stars.

Costar Wars—actors flinging dirt at former costars.

Directors' Cuts—directors cutting stars down to size and actors skewering directors (equal time here).

Let's Get Physical!—stars commenting on fellow stars' anatomies.

My ground rule for *Hollywood Babble On* was that each quote should be by one star about another star (or stars). In this, it is a first. Amid the star babble, an occasional positive piece of gossip creeps in. Excuse it. Now and then a compliment is bound to happen, even in Hollywood. (And a few of the couples in the "Exes" chapter are still together.)

A note about quotes: You may read one here that you've heard or read elsewhere, and it may differ by a word or two. This is because the more famous the quote, the more it might vary from source to source. A star may change or embroider a phrase in repeating an anecdote. He or she may take credit for someone else's quote or adapt it to her or his own usage. For example, in one of her stage shows Bette Midler declared of Britain's Princess Anne: "She loves nature in spite of what it did to her." In this collection, Forrest Tucker uses the same thought—inadvertently or not—but about an American subject.

The times may influence word usage. Groucho Marx's famous comparison of Victor Mature's and Hedy Lamarr's chests in one source used "bust"; in another, "tits." A quote is a quote, but like the stars themselves, not every quote is immutable over time and media.

At least with star quotes the public never need feel guilty, since *they* said it. And if they dished it out, they can be made to take it, too. The stars give as good as they get!

Even if much of what is said about some of the luminaries in this collection is a bit nasty, don't feel bad. For the stars are rich, famous, live like royalty, and are used to it. The barbs go with the gold-veined territory. Criticism is the tax one pays on fame.

So if scandal is to your taste, sit back and enjoy the feast.

October 5, 1993
Beverly Hills

Bette Davis (portrait by Sue Kutosh)

☆ ☆ ☆ ☆

In the Slimelight

☆ ☆ ☆ ☆

There are no heroes today. Name *one*. Michael Jackson?
—Bette Davis

☆ ☆ ☆ ☆

Who is this Miss Madonna? The idea that she would make a film from my *Blue Angel* is outrageous! She's no angel—on the contrary!
—Marlene Dietrich

☆ ☆ ☆ ☆

Shirley MacLaine—who does she think she isn't?
—Yves Montand

☆ ☆ ☆ ☆

Shirley MacLaine's the sort of liberal that if she found out who she was going to be in her next life, she'd make a will and leave all her money to herself.
—director Colin Higgins

1

Mel Gibson is somewhere to the right of Attila the Hun. He's beautiful, but only on the outside.

—Susan Sarandon

☆ ☆ ☆ ☆

[Charlton] Heston, he has an ego the size of Texas and a talent the size of South Dakota. *Why not North Dakota?* We won't go into that....

—Sal Mineo

☆ ☆ ☆ ☆

Charlton Heston has a bad memory. He still thinks he's Moses parting the Red Sea.

—Barbara Stanwyck

☆ ☆ ☆ ☆

He's the kind of guy that when he dies, he's going up to heaven and give God a bad time for making him bald.

—Marlon Brando on Frank Sinatra

☆ ☆ ☆ ☆

A Steve McQueen performance just naturally lends itself to monotony. Steve doesn't bring much to the party.

—Robert Mitchum

☆ ☆ ☆ ☆

Andy Warhol was a very lucky man. He couldn't paint, couldn't dress, couldn't talk. Even so, he became famous and obscenely rich. Who says that talent pays?

—Paulette Goddard

☆ ☆ ☆ ☆

Richard Burton complained that the papparazzi of Rome were following him into the public lavatories. The solution was not to retreat from view but to learn to urinate with style!

—Quentin Crisp

My daughter Nastassja Kinski has never forgiven me. For what, I don't know, because for years, she won't speak to me. She blackens my name in the press and makes me think abortion is an excellent idea.

—actor Klaus Kinski

☆ ☆ ☆ ☆

Jodie Foster is the type of so-called feminist only Camille Paglia could love.... Foster is too eager to please, and she wants people to really, really like her. What a pity.

—Germaine Greer

☆ ☆ ☆ ☆

Adele Astaire was the star of the family...so talented. Of course, then came marriage [and retirement]. Fred was...a bit cocky. Very American—you know, he had so little, yet so confident. But as for film stardom, who could have imagined it?

—Cecil Beaton

☆ ☆ ☆ ☆

Those were *B*-movies. If he [Ronald Reagan] had been in *Casablanca*, he wouldn't have become governor and president.... If he'd been married to his current wife [instead of] a successful actress [Jane Wyman], his ego could have handled not being a top-flight star. People like Reagan...lived quite well, nonetheless. But there wasn't much of a chance for a big breakthrough. Once in B-pictures, always in B-pictures.

—George Cukor

☆ ☆ ☆ ☆

He certainly doesn't publicize it now, but in the 1950s, John Wayne was one of the biggest Hollywood supporters, financially, of the Ku Klux Klan.

—Ralph Bellamy

☆ ☆ ☆ ☆

Rex Reed—he's either at your feet or at your throat.

—Ava Gardner

He doesn't overact, he doesn't underact. With him, it's no sweat. His real energies go into reading too many scripts and saying yes too often.

—Ralph Bellamy on Michael Caine

☆ ☆ ☆ ☆

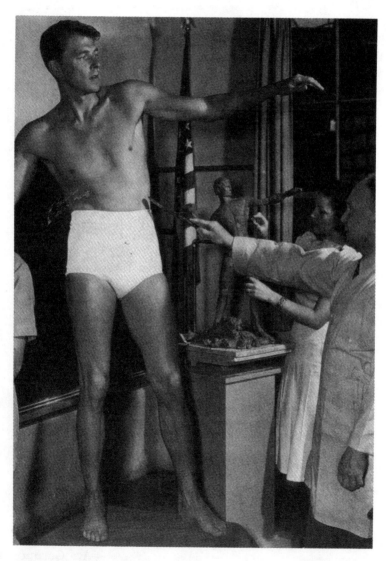

Ronald Reagan: Them thar hips

Elvis wasn't really anything but autosexual. He loved himself, and he loved cars.

—Keenan Wynn on Elvis Presley

☆ ☆ ☆ ☆

Mr. Warmth, he ain't. He's a loner. Whether that's on account of having been roommates with Al Gore in college, I don't know. They're both rather robotic, and they're both actors. Only, Gore plays heroes and Jones plays villains.

—director James Bridges on Tommy Lee Jones

☆ ☆ ☆ ☆

With Ryan O'Neal, what you see is all you get. That's why he won't be a star by 1985.

—Tom Tryon

☆ ☆ ☆ ☆

Ray Sharkey was one of Hollywood's most notorious drug addicts, and he died of AIDS. What's so ludicrous is how worried he and his handlers were that the public might think he wasn't heterosexual once they found out he had AIDS. Like abusing drugs is worse than loving your own kind!

—Boy George

☆ ☆ ☆ ☆

These fellows like Kirk Douglas and Chuck Heston who've played so many historical heroes, they can get pretty high and mighty. If you don't treat them like royalty, they get hurt or angry. They're happiest when you treat them like a king and act like a humble serf.

—Fred MacMurray

☆ ☆ ☆ ☆

Winning an Academy Award for Best Actor no longer makes a career. You don't believe me? Do you remember F. Murray Abraham? He won for *Amadeus*. And I'm the only one who remembers that!

—Trevor Howard

In my day, the leading men had substance. You could imagine them as real-life heroes. Now they're just a bunch of faces with bad attitude. Look at Mel Gibson. He's basically an overgrown, pretty-boy bully. He's not heroic, he has no charm, he's cardboard. I can't imagine him doing any of his own stunts. They keep saying the glamour is gone from today's celebrities, but so is the integrity and decency.

—John Lund

☆ ☆ ☆ ☆

If that child had been born in the Middle Ages, she'd have been burned as a witch.

—Lionel Barrymore on Margaret O'Brien

☆ ☆ ☆ ☆

Do I subscribe to the Olivier school of acting? Ah, nuts. I'm an actor. I just do what comes naturally.

—Humphrey Bogart

☆ ☆ ☆ ☆

Larry Olivier is not an actor. He's a chameleon. He wears all that makeup and all those costumes and just disguises himself. Half the time you don't even know it's him.

—Bette Davis

☆ ☆ ☆ ☆

I don't like the Hollywood definition of an actor. I like people who can act. The so-called Rock Hudsons and Tab Hunters are a dull bunch of cruds....Too many actors in Hollywood only think about their next part and about what Louella Parsons will say about them.

—Humphrey Bogart

☆ ☆ ☆ ☆

Brando? Actors like him are good, but on the whole I do not enjoy actors who seek to commune with their armpits, so to speak.

—Greer Garson

Method acting's an abomination. The chief lesson young actors from these so-called modern schools learn is complete egotism. They are taught to relate everything to self....Marlon Brando has been known to place rubber stoppers in his ears so he cannot hear the words spoken by other players!

—Boris Karloff

☆ ☆ ☆ ☆

Mr. Marlon Brando got, for an aggregate of twenty minutes on the screen in *Superman* and *Apocalypse Now*, more money than Clark Gable got for twenty years at M-G-M.

—Billy Wilder

☆ ☆ ☆ ☆

Rod Steiger's the worst actor that ever lived. The very name makes me throw up. He's so terrible. He's one of the world's worst hams. A real *jambon*!

—Truman Capote

☆ ☆ ☆ ☆

Michael Caine has lost any prestige that his Britishness conferred on him. He is the McDonald's of moviemaking. Now he goes for sheer quantity. He must figure there's safety in numbers—if you make eight or nine movies a year, one of them is bound to be a hit.

—Judith Anderson

☆ ☆ ☆ ☆

Jackie Gleason wasn't big enough for pictures. He became a star on the small screen. I worked with him, and I know—he was just a big bully. He had one emotion he could play: outrage. He was as false as his teeth. They call him the Great One; to many of us, he's merely the Overweight One.

—Betty Grable

☆ ☆ ☆ ☆

Kevin Costner is like Oakland: there is no there there.

—Marcello Mastroianni

Cockney sweater: Michael Caine

☆ ☆ ☆ ☆

Roseanne Barr is to television what Kate Smith was to radio. Unfortunately, TV is a visual medium, and by *medium*, I do mean half-baked.

—Vince Gardenia

Paul Newman's a great-looking ice cube.

—Sal Mineo

☆ ☆ ☆ ☆

I'm proud of being a wop....I was unique. They made all the guys change names, and half of them had to have nose jobs, like Dean Martin, alias Dino Crocetti. And the girls: Anne Bancroft's real name was Italiano—and Paula Prentiss's was Ragusa....We ain't all olive-skinned. Look at Connie Stevens or Bernadette Peters.

—Sal Mineo

☆ ☆ ☆ ☆

You had to stand in line to hate him.

—Hedda Hopper on Columbia mogul Harry Cohn

☆ ☆ ☆ ☆

It proves what they always say: Give the public what they want and they'll come out for it.

—Red Skelton at Cohn's crowded funeral

☆ ☆ ☆ ☆

Jack Warner would rather tell a bad joke than make a good movie. He'd give anything to be a comedian, and he doesn't realize that he is.

—Jack Benny

☆ ☆ ☆ ☆

Louis B. Mayer was a Jewish Hitler, a Fascist. Had no feeling for any minority, including his own. No feeling for people, period. When he found out that M-G-M contract player Lew Ayres was a conscientious objector, he was furious. He informed everyone that "Lew Ayres has some kind of a phobia about killing people." And he killed Lew's career.

—Ralph Bellamy

☆ ☆ ☆ ☆

Mr. Mayer could not believe my cousin [Ramón Novarro] was homosexual. He did not really know what a homosexual was. He felt that if he forced Ramón to marry, he could convert him. Ramón refused, saying his private life was his own. You can imagine what happened to Ramón's standing at Metro after that....

—Dolores Del Rio

☆ ☆ ☆ ☆

Noel Coward...acted just like an adult. Even then, I could see he would go far....A few times, he came to tea, but one time we both jumped up and down on the furniture, and my mother was furious. She said, "You are never to ask that boy to tea again. He has no manners and will never amount to anything." Noel and I were very friendly as children. However, as adults we drifted apart, because by then we each needed to be the complete center of attention.

—Hermione Gingold

☆ ☆ ☆ ☆

One critic called me Hormone Gingold, [but] I did impressions and ribbed the stars. For instance: "Oh, look, there's Florence Desmond doing an imitation of John Gielgud. Oh, no, it *is* John Gielgud." I was like Joan Rivers, but long before her. In those pretelevision days, it was thought very daring of us to poke fun at the stars by name.

—Hermione Gingold

☆ ☆ ☆ ☆

Elvis Presley gave me the only dinner party I've ever heard of his giving, in Las Vegas....We saw [his] opening show....I can't say that I was at all impressed by his performance. So we went down to this apartment he had there in the hotel, and the dinner party consisted of about eight young men and one old friend of mine—Doris Duke. This table was full of orchids up and down, and everything looked very fancy in a gauche, peculiar way. The dinner was...fried pork and fried chicken and fried catfish....He was nice; I sort of liked Elvis.

—Truman Capote

If I had stayed in Hollywood, I would have ended up like Alan Ladd [a suicide] and Gail Russell [who died from alcoholism], dead and buried. That rat race killed them, and I knew it eventually would kill me....I left to save my life.

—Veronica Lake

☆ ☆ ☆ ☆

Did you ever catch him at a funeral? It's wonderful. All through the years he makes notes on his friends. He wants to be ready.

—Eddie Cantor on George Jessel, Hollywood's unofficial eulogist

☆ ☆ ☆ ☆

I'm not a Richard Gere–type actor. I won't, to bring in a certain audience, jump in the sack and display nudity. If you want to see that, you can go buy a pornographic movie.

—Chuck Norris

☆ ☆ ☆ ☆

What ever happened to John Travolta? I heard he either joined some cult [Scientology] and got fat. Or he married and had a child. Which amounts to the same thing.

—Gérard Depardieu

☆ ☆ ☆ ☆

Errol Flynn says he doesn't worry about money as long as he can reconcile his net income with his gross habits.

—Sheilah Graham

☆ ☆ ☆ ☆

The son of a bitch is a ballet dancer! He's the best ballet dancer that ever lived, and if I get a good chance, I'll strangle him with my bare hands.

—W.C. Fields after viewing a Charlie Chaplin movie

☆ ☆ ☆ ☆

The trouble with Cecil is that he always bites off more than he can chew—and then chews it.

—director and brother William DeMille

☆ ☆ ☆ ☆

Think what Warren Beatty could have achieved if he'd been celibate!

—sister Shirley MacLaine

☆ ☆ ☆ ☆

I dated Warren Beatty. It was more publicity than I bargained for. But not so fulfilling. He is like a masculine dumb blonde.

—Anouk Aimée

☆ ☆ ☆ ☆

Cary Grant had charm, and that was about all. He was cold, paranoid, and cheap. You know who else was very cheap? Gable. They must have had wretchedly poor childhoods. Now, these two were not by any means close friends, but every December twenty-sixth, they called each other on the telephone and ar-ranged to meet that same week so they could exchange any monogrammed gifts they had received which they didn't want, because they shared the same initials!

—Capucine

☆ ☆ ☆ ☆

You can keep the pretty party boys. They're just for show. I like a man who can make me laugh. Looks fade, but a sense of humor is for keeps. I'll take a Woody Allen over a Warren Beauty [sic] any day!

—Bette Midler

☆ ☆ ☆ ☆

Woody Allen's universe, his movies, it's a closed little world. His movies don't contain any people of color or gays, and he is more interested in Lolitas than independent, exciting women. I think he has not progressed much beyond the 1960s.

—Catherine Deneuve

Woody Allen...is evil.
>—Maureen O'Sullivan (Mia Farrow's mother)

☆ ☆ ☆ ☆

My family are Republicans, going way, way back. That didn't mean what it means now. These days, it means people like Ronald Reagan, who was an unassuming Democrat until his wife got after him....I understand Reagan used to be a model in art school in his youth and that even then he was broad-hipped and narrow-minded.
>—Lillian Gish

☆ ☆ ☆ ☆

I once saw Kirk Douglas refuse to give an autograph to a little girl. He was irate and turned to an associate and shrugged, "I need this?" Charming....
>—Ralph Bellamy

☆ ☆ ☆ ☆

There are two brands of sadists in Hollywood. The real thing, a healthy sadist, like Bette Davis. Or a sadomasochist, like Joan Crawford, who was sadistic to some, including her kids, and masochistic in other quarters. Joan was not consistent. I mean, who would want to be a masochist? In Hollywood, it's always smarter to be a sadist.
>—Agnes Moorehead

☆ ☆ ☆ ☆

Orson Welles should have played in *The Man Who Came to Dinner*. As a houseguest, he was a nightmare! He completely took over the house, no request or demand was too big for him to make, and he sincerely believed he was bestowing a blessing by his very presence. Sheesh! I'd hate to have his nerve in my tooth.
>—Lucille Ball

☆ ☆ ☆ ☆

Nobody remembers Dana Andrews. He was a big star, interesting, he had plenty of personality and enough talent. He finally

Girth and mirth: Orson Welles and Lucille Ball

drowned his career in a bottle. What makes somebody do that? He was a *star*. I can understand it maybe if a failure does it, if somebody poor does it. But not a *star*.

—Peter Finch

☆ ☆ ☆ ☆

Hedda and Louella would have been jokes except for their power. Thank God no one in Hollywood today has that power. Now you have the Hollywood Kids as gossips. They're rather ridiculous, like those old bags were, but at least they have no power. Claws but no power!

—Jim Backus (*Gilligan's Island*)

☆ ☆ ☆ ☆

Merv Griffin sings like I look.

—Totie Fields

Arnold Schwarzenegger is a farce. In a more sophisticated culture, he would have remained a body cultist. In America, he is not only a movie star, he has political power. The son of a Nazi, yet what the father did should be separate from what the son does. But this Schwarzenegger, he invites the ex-Nazi president of Austria [Kurt Waldheim] to his wedding with a girl who is of the Kennedy family, a family of Democrats! He has no shame and no sense of what is appropriate or decent.

—Yves Montand

☆ ☆ ☆ ☆

Franco Zeffirelli began as my protégé. In time, he became a director. However, I do not like when they compare us—as directors or as men or Italians—for we are totally different, and I am convinced he joined the right wing to spite me. I am rich, of the nobility, and of the Left. He was born illegitimate, poor, then joined the bigots. He hates Jews, thinks women who have abortions should be put to death, and his attitudes and fanaticism are like a fundamentalist Moslem. And I do deny that he was my lover....

—Luchino Visconti

☆ ☆ ☆ ☆

George Jessel billed himself as the Toastmaster General of the United States and claimed that he never in his adult life ate lunch or dinner at home. That's because he was a champion freeloader!

—Jim Backus

☆ ☆ ☆ ☆

George Jessel was this big hypocrite. On the one hand, he pretended to uphold America's great institutions and morals, and on the other, he had probably the most renowned and extensive collection of pornography in Hollywood. Still and all, I guess pornography *is* a great American institution.

—Lee Marvin

☆ ☆ ☆ ☆

Merle Oberon went Hollywood before she went to Hollywood. She would do anything and everything to become a star. That included passing off her own mother, who was from India, as her maid. That's when Merle was in England, marrying her way up. Then she went to Hollywood and shed her Jewish husband and married a cameraman so she could look beautiful via an interested expert, because her half-Indian complexion caused her great difficulties on-screen. Of course by the time she arrived in Hollywood, her mother had died and been buried in an unmarked grave, part of Merle's hidden, secret past.

—James Mason

☆ ☆ ☆ ☆

Benny Hill could give female impersonators a bad name. I don't know or care what his real situation is, sexually, but he lives like a slob and he's wary of the media. He has an awful temper and becomes furious if asked if he is gay. If that makes him so irate, I would think he should find another profession. It's the same with that singer Michael Jackson. He goes out of his way to look, act, and sound like a young white lady, then gets all bent out of shape if people assume he'd rather be white or female. What are these chaps, nuts?

—Trevor Howard

☆ ☆ ☆ ☆

John Gielgud is the biggest gossip I know, and I know several. He's a fabulous talent, has a magnificent voice, and he's the first to admit that he is selfish and egocentric. How refreshing!

—Ralph Richardson

☆ ☆ ☆ ☆

They call her Attila the nun.

—Barbara Stanwyck on Loretta Young

☆ ☆ ☆ ☆

When she was young, Loretta was pretty. That, not her talent, got her cast in film after film. Cecil B. DeMille told me the story of his directing her in *The Crusades*. She was doing a scene, urging Richard the Lion-Hearted to go to the Middle East and fight. Nothing like today's Middle East! Loretta read her line: "Richard, you gotta save Christianity!" But not very convincingly. So DeMille took her aside and asked her to put some awe into her line reading. They reshot the scene, and she said, "Aw, Richard, you gotta save Christianity!

—David Niven

☆ ☆ ☆ ☆

Nelson Eddy has personality-minus.

—Louis B. Mayer

☆ ☆ ☆ ☆

Kevin Costner has personality-minus.

—Madonna

☆ ☆ ☆ ☆

Hollywood is all façade. Actresses like Jeanette MacDonald and Grace Kelly pretended they were madonnas but were really sluts. And now you have a slut named Madonna! I'm not putting her down, though. Most of the men in Hollywood are sluts, too.

—John Cassavetes

☆ ☆ ☆ ☆

They called Jeanette MacDonald the Iron Butterfly and Nelson Eddy the Singing Capon. She was a conservative priss who in real life had several lovers, while he played screen lovers, had one wife, and showed little or no sexual interest in her!

—Joan Blondell

☆ ☆ ☆ ☆

My novel *Travels With My Aunt* was retooled for Maggie Smith, who shrieked and flailed her way through the movie version. It was not a performance without merit; however, it is the same one I've seen in most of her pictures.

—Graham Greene

☆ ☆ ☆ ☆

Richard Gere is the crankiest actor I've met. He doesn't smile; he leers. Not exactly an intellectual, either....For a while, that dropping-his-pants bit was an effective gimmick for the screen, but any way you measure it, his talent isn't big enough.

—Cornel Wilde

Ali MacGraw is proof that a great model is not necessarily a great, or even an average, actress.

—Peter Sellers

☆ ☆ ☆ ☆

What ever happened to Joan Crawford? I mean, *before* she became a star. For decades, there were rumors she'd been a call girl or did stag movies. I suppose it's too late ever to find out. Once you're a star, the image takes over, and they go and write a biomythography of you....

—Rudy Vallee

☆ ☆ ☆ ☆

Gig Young....I'd meet him at parties now and then, and one time I jokingly asked if Gig was short for *gigolo*. He became furious but tried not to show it. But if looks could kill, I wouldn't be here today. Lucky it was in public. He coolly informed me that his real name was Byron Barr....I did hear he had quite a temper, which he rarely displayed. But then he really let it gain the upper hand when he got mad at his wife and shot her, then shot himself. I'm just glad I didn't ask him about his name in private!

—Geraldine Page

☆ ☆ ☆ ☆

Yes, it's true. Tom Selleck and Paulina Porizkova did have a feud while making *Her Alibi*. But I can't tell you why she had an antipathy for him. In Hollywood, you can get sued for telling the truth. After all, it's Hollywood where the truth lies....

—Anthony Perkins

☆ ☆ ☆ ☆

Engelbert Humperdinck is a gimmick. Whatever his real name is, his manager gave him that name as a gimmick. It's the same guy who managed Tom Jones, and *he* was named after the Oscar-winning movie *Tom Jones*, from the Fielding novel. At least Jones is a normal name and the guy has a voice worth listening to.

—Ray Milland, né Reginald Truscott-Jones

I did *not* give Lee Majors his start in acting. You can't pin that one on me. Technically, he hasn't started acting yet. He had a pretty face, then he got a pretty wife [Farrah Fawcett], now he has a pretty career.

—Rock Hudson

☆ ☆ ☆ ☆

Donna Mills is a TV actress. Period. She's not big enough for the big screen, even with those painted-on eyes. She even did a video on how to make your eyes seem bigger! From Jane Fonda to this! It's idiotic. Now they'll make videos on any subject that'll grab the attention span of a few hundred bored housewives who watch too much TV.

—Cornel Wilde

☆ ☆ ☆ ☆

Keir Dullea, gone tomorrow.

—Noel Coward

☆ ☆ ☆ ☆

Maurice Chevalier helped choose me for my first leading movie role, and I do not wish to speak unkindly of the man. I did not while he was alive. But it's amusing, and quite misleading, that so many people came to think of him as an extravagant French lover. In reality, he was a notorious tightwad, and his career was the only lover I ever saw.

—Frances Dee

☆ ☆ ☆ ☆

Ricardo Montalban is to improvisational acting what Mount Rushmore is to animation.

—John Cassavetes

☆ ☆ ☆ ☆

Fred MacMurray just might be the cheapest, most self-centered actor in Hollywood. I say "might" because I want to leave some legal room for doubt. Nah, he'd never sue me. He's too goddamned cheap!

—William (*I Love Lucy*) Frawley

Richard Attenborough did what most middling actors dream of doing—he became a director. All of a sudden, he gives the orders, and he looks good because he's behind the camera, not in front of it.

—Michael Bennett

☆ ☆ ☆ ☆

People think what they see on TV is reality. That's why everyone thought Arthur Godfrey was the salt of the earth. More like salt in your coffee! Ask anyone who ever worked with him—he was one of the meanest, pettiest, most rotten-souled performers, and I do mean performers, that ever worked on television or any other medium.

—Wally Cox

☆ ☆ ☆ ☆

Lucy likes to take charge, but her temper's not as black as—should I say as *red* as her hair! Or, for that matter, as Arthur Godfrey's!

—Vivian Vance

☆ ☆ ☆ ☆

Michael Landon can be a spoiled brat when he wants to be, and he often wants to be.

—David Janssen

☆ ☆ ☆ ☆

I did a charity function with Landon once. He was smiley and affable while the camera was on him, but boy, the second it turned off, he didn't have time for anyone except the other VIPs in the room.

—Nancy Walker

☆ ☆ ☆ ☆

Elvis was the kind of white-trash-turned-star that, when the Beatles came along, he called them sissies or Communists because they knocked him right out of the limelight.

—Johnnie Ray

Elvis on his fake surfboard

Elvis was the Pelvis. That's what we had to call him then. Actually, Elvis was the Penis....

—Diana Dors

☆ ☆ ☆ ☆

Elvis Presley was not a deep thinker. He went by stereotypes. He thought blond hair belonged to girls, and dumb girls at that, so he changed his hair color. Dyed it black, to be somewhat more macho and intelligent.

—John Lennon

☆ ☆ ☆ ☆

Bruce Lee was an egomaniac. He thought it was terrible that he had to be just a movie star when what he really wanted to be was a dictator. I'm not kidding. He wanted to rule China or Taiwan or somewhere!

—Lee Marvin

☆ ☆ ☆ ☆

Natalie Wood played Maria, the Puerto Rican damsel in *West Side Story*. Natalie lost.

—Leonard Bernstein

☆ ☆ ☆ ☆

Natalie is sweet, though she's a born exhibitionist. She grew up in the business, from a child star. But she's never had the dramatic presence that Elizabeth Taylor, also a former child star, has. Natalie cannot do drama very well. She knows and accepts this…and when Harvard's Hasty Pudding Club named her the worst actress of the year, she was so excited by all the publicity, and all she could think of was, what was she going to wear?

—Jeffrey Hunter

☆ ☆ ☆ ☆

Natalie Wood will be sensational in *Gypsy*. She plays a stripper.

—Rosalind Russell

☆ ☆ ☆ ☆

The coldest man in movies was George Sanders. Oh, not on the screen. In real life. In real life, he made his movie characters seem sentimental.

—Anne Baxter

Jerome Robbins may be a talented choreographer, but he is no mensch. It's thanks to people like him that Jack Gilford and I and countless others were blacklisted during the McCarthy era. I

Natalie Wood—and could!

never thought, during the 1950s, that someday I'd ever work with Jerome Robbins. I also never thought I'd ever work again, period.

—Zero Mostel

☆ ☆ ☆ ☆

David Janssen screwed more women in Hollywood than Kennedy screwed in Washington, Hollywood, and everywhere else combined!

—John Wayne

☆ ☆ ☆ ☆

I always heard W. C. Fields was impotent and that he took it out in drink.

—Freddie Bartholomew

☆ ☆ ☆ ☆

Yes, I have acted with Clint Eastwood. Or rather, I have acted opposite Clint Eastwood.

—Geraldine Page

☆ ☆ ☆ ☆

Gerry Page is a superb Method actress. I once asked what method she used. She said, without batting an eyelash, "Talent."

—Helen Hayes

☆ ☆ ☆ ☆

I've never known anyone in Hollywood as talkative as Miss Page. I suppose that is why she lives in New York. With theater, you get to repeat yourself every night.

—Laurence Harvey

☆ ☆ ☆ ☆

Cary Grant didn't give a damn about anyone but himself. That man wouldn't stick his neck out for anyone. Myrna Loy and I tried to get him to join the stars who were speaking out against the political witchhunts. He refused to say anything or sign anything, didn't even wish us good luck....Another time, a friend of mine was in a five-and-dime in Los Angeles, waiting in a long line. Grant came in, picked up some items, looked at the line, mumbled, then asked out loud if he couldn't move to the head of the line, because he was "in a hurry." Naturally, they let him go to the head of the line. Who's going to refuse Cary Grant? People idolize without knowing who or what they're worshiping.

—Melvyn Douglas

☆ ☆ ☆ ☆

It's so silly, this martyrdom of St. Frances Farmer. Everyone states that she was ruined by the movie business, but she just wasn't cut out for it. She came to Hollywood knowing the rules but chose to flout them. She was self-destructive, but because she fought her battles in Hollywood, she got more publicity, and because she was beautiful, they've canonized her. She was not bad, but neither was she an innocent victim. Nobody in Hollywood is innocent!

—Cary Grant

☆ ☆ ☆ ☆

They say that sex symbols die young or they are the products of miserable childhoods or they're purportedly frigid. Who really knows? All I know is that the two most self-destructive girls in Hollywood were beautiful blondes—Frances Farmer and Marilyn Monroe. The nonblondes do seem to be better survivors....

—Richard Burton

☆ ☆ ☆ ☆

Richard Burton could have been another Olivier, but he met Elizabeth Taylor. He went Hollywood after marrying Dame Fortune.

—Judith Anderson

☆ ☆ ☆ ☆

Laurence Olivier is the most overrated actor on earth. Take away the wives and the looks, and you have John Gielgud.

—Oscar Levant

Those movie goddesses like Garbo and Crawford, they probably never had children because it might ruin their figures....Crawford wanted it both ways. She wanted the publicity. So she adopted. Someone like that, you figure she does everything for publicity. Her whole life is a false front. Or at least a well-padded one.

—Oscar Levant

☆ ☆ ☆ ☆

I happen to know that Tallulah Bankhead and Joan Crawford couldn't have babies because of the illegal abortions performed on them. This was a major, scandalous topic of conversation and gossip in show biz circles in the old days. Those good old days weren't!

—Veronica Lake

☆ ☆ ☆ ☆

Walter Brennan is a crotchety old cuss! As for his politics, don't ask. He makes John Wayne look like a liberal.

—Randolph Scott

☆ ☆ ☆ ☆

José Ferrer is ashamed of his heritage. That's because he is not handsome enough to be a Latin Lover, and so he shies away from being labeled a Latin. I don't mind—I am a handsome Latin and a wonderful lover!

—Fernando Lamas

☆ ☆ ☆ ☆

For a long time, there was this erroneous rumor makin' the rounds that Dinah Shore is of "mixed" ancestry [part black]. I don't know how that particular rumor got started....The truth is, she's Jewish. But she don't talk about that, either, honey.

—Moms Mabley

☆ ☆ ☆ ☆

Ronald Colman is a gentleman. Yes, yes. So big deal! He's also a regular sleeping pill. Zzz....

—Van Heflin

Broderick Crawford represents a backlash against the good-looking younger actors. He can play a hero or a heavy. What he can't play is a skinny. Now, I don't object to his portly, surly manner, but the fellow's got no class. What the hell happened to gentlemen like Ronald Colman and David Niven? Is this the best America can do?

—George Sanders

☆ ☆ ☆ ☆

I loved William Holden, but I could not have knowingly married an alcoholic.

—Audrey Hepburn

☆ ☆ ☆ ☆

I once saw a photograph of W. C. Fields and his drinking partner John Barrymore sitting at a table with a cup of coffee in front of each. I knew it was a posed photo because of the coffee....

—Peter Finch

☆ ☆ ☆ ☆

I won an Academy Award for *Ben-Hur*. I was classically trained, worked all my life, did theater, worked with the best. Then I appeared in that rather pretentious picture, which was something of a bloated popular epic, yet it won numerous Oscars, and so did Charlton Heston in it. That somewhat deflated the value of my own award, in terms of achievement, don't you think?

—Hugh Griffith

☆ ☆ ☆ ☆

It's hard to believe Anna Magnani won the Academy Award [for *The Rose Tattoo*] and not Susan Hayward! Shouldn't they have separate categories for foreigners? I mean, they're called the Oscars, not the Raviolis.

—Ward Bond

☆ ☆ ☆ ☆

The name sounded familiar, but I didn't realize I had worked with him....

—Joan Crawford on Ward Bond, a supporting actor in *Johnny Guitar*

John Wayne and his drinking buddy Ward Bond went around wrecking careers with their gung-ho willingness to blacklist anyone who politically disagreed with them during the 1950s.

—Melvyn Douglas

☆ ☆ ☆ ☆

The way I heard it, when Pearl Harbor was attacked, Joan Crawford was on the set, in her chair, knitting. Someone rushed over to the set and yelled, "The Japanese have destroyed Pearl Harbor!" Joan looked up and said, "Oh, dear. Who was she?"

—Mary Astor

☆ ☆ ☆ ☆

Paul Scofield is one Best Actor [for *A Man for All Seasons*] the Oscar won't help. He does have talent but not star quality. Ten years from now, who will remember him?

—Curt Jurgens

☆ ☆ ☆ ☆

F. Murray Abraham is the Oscar-winning Best Actor [for *Amadeus*] this year. But will the public know him a year from now?

—Trevor Howard

☆ ☆ ☆ ☆

The way it's going, you'd think the Academy [of Motion Picture Arts and Sciences] was composed of doctors. Liz Taylor wins for a tracheotomy, and Patricia Neal wins for a brain tumor. I do feel sorry for them, but I'm thinking my smartest career move might be a serious illness instead of a good role.

—Anne Baxter

☆ ☆ ☆ ☆

Are we honestly supposed to believe that the Academy Awards are for acting ability when John Wayne has won the Oscar but Richard Burton, umpteen nominations and all, hasn't?

—Vic Morrow

Winning the Oscar signifies many things, not least among them the fact that I no longer have to be known in Hollywood as Hayley Mills's father.

—John Mills

☆ ☆ ☆ ☆

Best Actor today, forgotten tomorrow: F. Murray Abraham

If Ginger Rogers [Best Actress for *Kitty Foyle*] is an actress, so am I.

—Oscar Levant

☆ ☆ ☆ ☆

Look at today's Academy Award winners, though. Diane Keaton, Richard Dreyfuss....They look like my ex-neighbors! And even my ex-neighbors dress better.

—Cornel Wilde

☆ ☆ ☆ ☆

John Gielgud is so camp! When he took home his Oscar for *Arthur*, he said, "Just what I've always wanted—a naked man in my rumpus room."

—Liberace

☆ ☆ ☆ ☆

I was disappointed not to win [for *Victor/Victoria*]. But actors never win in gay roles [until William Hurt]. The Academy pats you on the back with a nomination; it's as if they're saying, "How brave of you," and, "Quite a stretch." But they can't help wondering about you if you play the role too well....

—Robert Preston

☆ ☆ ☆ ☆

If Cher can win an Oscar, I can become anorexic. There's truly hope. Bob Hope springs infernal in the Industry.

—Sam Kinison

☆ ☆ ☆ ☆

I think places like Palm Springs electing Sonny Bono mayor, and before that, Carmel with Clint Eastwood, it means those towns aren't really looking for leadership; they're looking for publicity.

—Nancy Walker

☆ ☆ ☆ ☆

I thought *Chariots of Fire* was a tedious, propagandistic film. How it ever won the Oscar is beyond me. I thought *Reds* was much more sweeping, impressive, and interesting, and I applauded Warren Beatty's victory as Best Director....John Gielgud was in *Chariots of Fire*, but he won for another picture. I think the music score swayed the voters....I think if one watches *Chariots of Fire* a second time, one realizes there is less there than meets the eye.

—*Chariots* star Ian Charleson

☆ ☆ ☆ ☆

Woody Allen didn't win the Academy Award just because of *Annie Hall*. He won it because he finally had a hit.

—George Burns

☆ ☆ ☆ ☆

Don Ameche got an award for break-dancing in *Cocoon*, only all his dancing was done by a stunt double. Doesn't the dancer deserve his own junior Oscar?

—James Coco

☆ ☆ ☆ ☆

Clint Eastwood and I will never win an Oscar. We're too popular.

—Burt Reynolds

☆ ☆ ☆ ☆

Ronald Reagan was destined never to win an Academy Award or become a top-ranked movie star. Which may be what it takes for certain men to become mayors or governors or presidents....Hitler wanted to be a painter, failed, and became a vindictive politician.

—Jean-Pierre Aumont

☆ ☆ ☆ ☆

Peter Finch was one of Britain's best actors. He'd won awards everywhere, from Moscow to London and Sydney. But not in Hollywood. They didn't give him an award [an Oscar, for *Network*] until he'd died!

—Peter Sellers

British actors are overrated. Ben Kingsley wins the Academy Award, and *Gandhi is* a good movie, but Kingsley got the part due to his resemblance to Gandhi. Because if you *are* going to hand these things out for resemblance or impersonation, then you have to give one to Faye Dunaway [in *Mommie Dearest*] as Joan Crawford....

—Yul Brynner

☆ ☆ ☆ ☆

How many Oscars does Katharine Hepburn need? She has, what, five? [Four.] Shouldn't she be put out of the running? Anyway, she's really not that different from role to role, and sentiment's a big factor in those Oscar decisions. Hepburn's still around, so the Oscars honor her just for dragging herself out of bed and putting on a turtleneck (in *On Golden Pond*) and showing up for work! Sure, she showed up. I would, too. Wouldn't you if you got an Oscar every time you got up to read the telephone book?

—José Ferrer

☆ ☆ ☆ ☆

How did Sally Field win two Oscars? I can name brilliant actresses who have never won one! Poor Henry Fonda finally wins one but is too sick to accept in person, and Katharine Hepburn will soon have enough Oscars to use them as bowling pins. It is too lopsided.

—Simone Signoret

☆ ☆ ☆ ☆

They call her Mama Mia. When we did *Rosemary's Baby*, she got pregnant by the devil. In real life, I think she's taken it too far. It's one thing to have a couple of kids, even three or four. But when most of the world's problems are caused by overpopulation, I have to shake my head over somebody who seems obsessed with kids as some sort of panacea for their personal problems or insecurities and keeps adding child after child to her tribe. I question what her psychology is and at what point she'll feel she has enough children....

—John Cassavetes

America never liked Josephine Baker. They didn't like that a Negro gal could go to France and there achieve a degree of stardom unavailable to her in this land.... What really pissed the columnists, like Walter Winchell, was her adopting all those kids of all races. They accused her of publicity-mongering...and others didn't want her raising white kids, but above all, they resented that she'd left America. What, she was supposed to stay here and become a maid?

—Dorothy Dandridge

☆ ☆ ☆ ☆

I read that Mr. [Frankie] Avalon has eight or nine children. I do not dare criticize, because a man of his celebrity can at least afford to rear so many screaming little tykes. Usually it is those who can least afford them that have the most offspring. Of course, having a child is an admission that a man requires help in making a name for himself. Michelangelo and Leonardo da Vinci never had children, yet I suspect that their names may be remembered long after those of my nephews or Mr. Avalon's children or Mr. Avalon himself are forgotten.

—Quentin Crisp

☆ ☆ ☆ ☆

Marilyn [Monroe] had this fantasy of having a child by Albert Einstein, whom she absolutely idolized. Marilyn converted to Judaism, you know, but it's not widely noted. Anyhow, Marilyn believed that between her and Einstein, they could have the perfect child—one with her looks and his brain. By another token, what if they had a child and it had Einstein's looks and Marilyn's brain?

—Otto Preminger

☆ ☆ ☆ ☆

Frank Sinatra is a seriously split personality. Conflicted, that is. First a Democrat, then a Republican. First he loved JFK, then he hated him. He once filmed an appeal to Americans during the war [WWII], asking them not to hate Jews and others who were minorities, and in the same spot he urges Americans to go out and kill "Japs" and win the war. Then he does this movie [*The*

Detective] where he's a cop but he's pro-gay—so already you know it's fiction—and next, Liz Taylor asks him to appear at the first big AIDS benefit, and he refuses 'cause he doesn't want to be associated with *that*....Inconsistency, thy name is Francis!

—James Coco

☆ ☆ ☆ ☆

I don't much care what people think, and neither does Frank Sinatra. Except when he does.

—Peter Lawford

☆ ☆ ☆ ☆

If Peter Lawford had been nicer to Marilyn [Monroe], she might be alive today. He's a creep.

—Danny Kaye

☆ ☆ ☆ ☆

I liked Peter [Lawford], I felt sorry for him. He aged so quickly. He was no angel, but who is? I was shocked when I read that after he died, his own children, those half-Kennedy children, wouldn't pay a penny toward his funeral! No matter what kind of father he was, that is shocking. If *my* children ever pulled that on me, I would come back and haunt them! Of course, I've been a very good mother and am not likely to die as broke as poor Peter did.

—Bette Davis

☆ ☆ ☆ ☆

I'm surprised none of the Kennedys have gone into show business. We have mediocre actors becoming politicians, but we never seem to have politicians turning their deceptive skills to the silver screen. I guess the only fictitious characters they like to portray are themselves.

—Truman Capote

☆ ☆ ☆ ☆

Hollywood's dumbest blonde never even made a Hollywood picture. It is Brigitte Bardot. She is—she was—beautiful in an overripe way. But she was and remains cheap, petty, jealous, bigoted, and untalented. She also tries to kill herself every few years, without success. I hope she never succeeds, but one wonders if she is very good at anything?

—Yves Montand

☆ ☆ ☆ ☆

Catherine Deneuve is an iceberg. Gorgeous, but an iceberg. And her beauty is melting, melting, melting....

—Steve McQueen

☆ ☆ ☆ ☆

Bob Hope would attend the opening of a supermarket.

—Marlon Brando

☆ ☆ ☆ ☆

Cesar Romero would attend the opening of a napkin.

—Jim Backus

☆ ☆ ☆ ☆

Yes, but Michael York would attend the opening of an envelope.

—Glenda Jackson

☆ ☆ ☆ ☆

I heard that before *Baby Jane*, when Bette Davis was washed up in the movies and took her act on the road, Tallulah Bankhead sent her a first-night telegram which read: Kisses on Your Opening.... Tallulah was AC-DC. Bette is strictly B.D.

—Joan Blondell

☆ ☆ ☆ ☆

Nowadays, the women are sexually aggressive, to an extreme, like Madonna, and the men are sexually passive or not at all, like Michael Jackson. Worst of all, the biggest stars in Hollywood now aren't even actors; they're singers whose voices are undistinguished and merely serviceable! What ever happened to class?

—Bette Davis

Jeremy Irons has no sex appeal. And not much sex, either. He's perfect for horror movies. Or science-fiction. He's an iceberg with an accent.

—Andy Warhol

☆ ☆ ☆ ☆

In the old days, the romantic symbols had individuality. Gable, Power, even George Brent at Warners. They were handsome, but they had personalities....Nowadays, the so-called sex symbols are made with cookie-cutters, they're all alike. On 'Beverly Hills 90210,' which I watched *once*, I can't tell the two boys apart. The one, they compare him to James Dean [Luke Perry]! The other, I don't know who they compare him [Jason Priestley] to. As far as I'm concerned, they should throw them both back in the pond. Neither is movie star material, even by today's lowered standards.

—Claudette Colbert

☆ ☆ ☆ ☆

When I was new to Hollywood, good manners were stressed. We were expected to be polite in public. That's all gone. Now, someone like Alec Baldwin behaves like a spoiled brat whenever he feels like it. Like, what's he so angry about? He's young, handsome, rich, famous. Isn't that enough?

—Anthony Perkins

☆ ☆ ☆ ☆

I was particularly stunned by the casting of [Tom] Cruise, who is no more my Vampire LeStat than Edward G. Robinson is Rhett Butler.
—Anne Rice on the filming of her novel *Interview With the Vampire*

☆ ☆ ☆ ☆

Will I have to be married to have kids? Maybe I won't be—just to piss off Dan Quayle.

—Geena Davis

It may be Hollywood's weirdest unexplained mystery—whatever happened to John Travolta?

—columnist Joyce Haber

☆ ☆ ☆ ☆

Beverly Hills is wonderful. The worst thing about it is that Andrew Dice Clay lives here.

—"Laugh-In" producer George Schlatter

☆ ☆ ☆ ☆

Kevin Costner....I call him personality-minus....Why do Americans keep trying to portray British characters? Costner as Robin Hood was ludicrous, and Mel Gibson as Hamlet was the rottenest something in Denmark in years! I know you Yanks think of him as Australian, but he's from the States, and Australians think of Gibson as an American.

—Frankie Howerd

☆ ☆ ☆ ☆

When my husband and I left to go to England right before *The Adventures of Ford Fairlane* came out, we said, "If it's a hit, we're not coming back." We were joking, but we weren't, really. Because if America had accepted Andrew Dice Clay's attitude toward women and gays and minorities and embraced that horrendous, horrific character, I don't think I could have lived here.

—Rita Rudner

☆ ☆ ☆ ☆

Meow!

☆ ☆ ☆ ☆

Shirley Temple had charisma as a child. But it cleared up as an adult.

—Totie Fields

☆ ☆ ☆ ☆

That horrible blond woman [Joan Rivers]? I couldn't be bothered paying any attention to anything she says about me.

—Elizabeth Taylor

☆ ☆ ☆ ☆

You know, once they're dead, death just scrubs [celebrities] clean. Everybody says, "Oh, they were wonderful." Suddenly, Grace Kelly didn't drink.

—Joan Rivers

☆ ☆ ☆ ☆

Mae West—she's a legend in her own mind.

—Jayne Mansfield

☆ ☆ ☆ ☆

I was on the set the day Mae West and Alison Skipworth were ready to play a scene. Skippy was edgy. She knew beforehand that Mae was going to steal it. When she could stand it no longer, she turned to Mae haughtily and said, "I'll have you know I'm an actress!" "It's all right," Mae said. "I'll keep your secret."

—Hedda Hopper

☆ ☆ ☆ ☆

They arrested Helen Reddy for loitering in front of an orchestra.

—Bette Midler

☆ ☆ ☆ ☆

I don't "get" Janis Joplin. That girl has problems....Bein' heard ain't one of 'em; like me, she gives an audience their money's worth. But when I sing, everything's comin' up roses. When she sings, it's a primal scream, for heaven's sake!

—Ethel Merman

☆ ☆ ☆ ☆

I was at a formal reception in New York, and you know Josephine Baker, the wonderful colored singer-dancer? American, born and bred, but there she was, acting majestic and using a French accent! Well, I'm not the formal type—at least not in the States. So then Miss Baker extended her gloved hand, as if she expected me to kiss it, and she drawled in English and French that it was a "grand plaisir" to meet me, "Lady Peel." So I smiled, shook her hand, and said, "Ah likes you too, honey."

—Beatrice Lillie

☆ ☆ ☆ ☆

Say anything you like, but don't say I love to work. That sounds like Mary Pickford, that prissy bitch.

—Mabel Normand at a press conference

☆ ☆ ☆ ☆

Bette Midler's a comic actress, but she missed her calling. She'd prefer to be a great tragedienne. She'll cry at the drop of a cue.

—Geraldine Page

Diane Keaton is no relation to the other famous Keaton. Although they should have switched names. She acts like a Buster, and he was male but very graceful—and always "Diane" for a laugh. Get it? Bad pun.

—Joan Hackett

☆ ☆ ☆ ☆

I've enjoyed wonderful health. The only time I ever got sick was when I watched Barbra Streisand in *Hello, Dolly!* on an airplane.
—Carol Channing, star of Broadway's *Hello, Dolly!* (Streisand starred in the movie)

☆ ☆ ☆ ☆

They've nicknamed her husband the Lizard of Roz, and what they call Rosalind Russell I can't repeat, but it does rhyme with "witch," and you'll find her sort in a kennel!
—Ethel Merman, star of Broadway's *Gypsy* (Russell starred in the movie.)

☆ ☆ ☆ ☆

When I worked with Katharine Hepburn, decades ago, I was terrified of her—that voice, her jaw, the whole package. I'm still scared of her!

—Lucille Ball

☆ ☆ ☆ ☆

[Katharine] Hepburn got the *role,* but *I* got the *guy* and the *baby* to go with him!
—Margaret Sullavan, star of the 1936 play *Stage Door;* in 1937, Hepburn starred in the film version, and Sullavan wed their agent, Leland Hayward, and gave birth to Brooke Hayward

☆ ☆ ☆ ☆

Lucille Ball was a control freak. Had to be in charge of everything. Never saw a woman who took her comedy so seriously.

—Phyllis Diller

[Appearing on *The Tonight Show* with Dinah Shore]: I think she must have gotten a bug up her posterior about my dress or something....Even though I didn't want to get low with an older woman on network television—an awful breach of etiquette—I was primed to let her have it: Look, you provincial prune, get out of my face!

—Angela Bowie

☆ ☆ ☆ ☆

Tallulah Bankhead is a marvelous female impersonator.

—Anne Baxter

☆ ☆ ☆ ☆

I remember Tallulah telling of going into a public ladies' room and discovering there was no toilet tissue. She looked underneath the booth and said to the lady in the next stall, "I beg your pardon, do you happen to have any toilet tissue in there?" The lady said no. So Tallulah said, "Well, then, dahling, do you have two fives for a ten?"

—Ethel Merman

☆ ☆ ☆ ☆

Mama [Judy Garland] and I were someplace like Lake Tahoe and went into the ladies' room. There was an old lady drunk there, and she said, "Oh, Judy, you're terrific. You got to always remember the rainbow." When Mama went into one of the stalls, the lady knocked on the door and said, "Judy, never forget the rainbow." Later on, she went up to Mama and went on and on again about her not forgetting the rainbow. Finally, Mama turned and said, "How can I forget the rainbow? I've got rainbows up my ass!"

—Liza Minnelli

☆ ☆ ☆ ☆

I once told Celeste Holm, "You're so lucky not to be a big Hollywood star, bound to a contract." Celeste is cool to me to this day.

—Joan Fontaine

I wish I *had* a sister. I've always been the intruder in her life, the interloper. As my older sibling, Olivia [de Havilland] could have looked after me. *Au contraire,* her desire my whole life has been to get me off-balance. We've not spoken since Mother's death in 1974, and that's it, kid. Never again.

—Joan Fontaine

☆ ☆ ☆ ☆

Joan deserved to win [the Oscar] and did. But Joan is fifteen months younger than I, and I knew I would lose prestige with her if I lost—I had always been a heroine in her eyes—and I did! The goddess had feet of clay, and she let me know it, too!

—Olivia de Havilland

☆ ☆ ☆ ☆

Everyone wants to know about the feud between my sister and myself, and why shouldn't I admit that I haven't been able to forgive her for not inviting me to our mother's memorial service…and for other cruelties. I married first, won the Oscar before Olivia did, and if I die first she'll undoubtedly be livid because I beat her to it.

—Joan Fontaine

☆ ☆ ☆ ☆

The first time I heard of Madonna, I thought she was a nun. Nowadays, people wonder, What has Madonna got? Has she got beauty, talent, charisma? The correct answer is: Nun of the Above.

—Joan Rivers

☆ ☆ ☆ ☆

Mrs. [Agatha] Christie said I was perhaps too portly to play her character Miss Marple. But I received not a single complaint from the filmgoers, and I think Mrs. Christie is a better novelist than she is a casting director.

—Margaret Rutherford

☆ ☆ ☆ ☆

When they asked Judith Anderson how becoming a dame had changed her life, she said she found that she wore gloves more often....I'm surprised she takes it so lightly—[being knighted] is a great honor, though I still don't like the word "dame" when it's pronounced by an American....

—Dame Peggy Ashcroft

☆ ☆ ☆ ☆

Joan Crawford—Hollywood's first case of syphilis.

—Bette Davis

☆ ☆ ☆ ☆

One area of life Joan should never have gotten into was children. She *bought* them....Joan was the perfect mother in front of the public but not behind the front door. She wanted this image that

JOAN CRAWFORD HATS
DESIGNED FOR AND POSED BY THE FAMOUS METRO-GOLDWYN-MAYER STAR

Your Choice

$1.95 Each

78N6603—Fits 21 to 21½ inches head size.
78N6604—Fits 21¾ to 22¼ inches head size.
Colors: **Kasha beige (light sand), navy blue or almond green. Measure and state color.** Shpg. wt., 1¾ lbs.
For the miss and young woman who prefer a hat with a brim, this genuine Joan Crawford model is an excellent choice. Good grade **full body felt** with unique appliqued design of Rayon embroidery floss in h a r m o n i z i n g shades. Grosgrain ribbon band.

78N6626—Fits 20¾ to 21¼ in. head size.
78N6627—Fits 21½ to 22 inches head size.
Colors: **French beige (sand), gobelin (medium) blue or Afghan (bright) red. Measure and state color.** Shipping weight, 1¾ pounds.
When it's a genuine Joan Crawford model you know the style is the latest. Good quality **full body felt.** Unusual brim drapes gracefully and forms flat trim at front. Novelty pin adds smart touch. Rayon lining. A wonderful value.

Joan Crawford: Do as I say, not as I did!

wasn't meant for her. I've never behaved like—Well, I doubt that *my* children will write a book.

—Bette Davis

☆ ☆ ☆ ☆

I don't hate Bette Davis even though the press wants me to. I resent her—I don't see how she built a career out of a set of mannerisms instead of real acting ability. Take away the pop eyes, the cigarette, and those funny clipped words and what have you got? She's phony, but I guess the public likes that.

—Joan Crawford

☆ ☆ ☆ ☆

Joan Crawford—I wouldn't sit on her toilet!

—Bette Davis

☆ ☆ ☆ ☆

I saw Bette Davis in a hotel in Madrid once and went up to her and said, "Miss Davis, I'm Ava Gardner and I'm a great fan of yours." And she behaved exactly as I wanted her to behave. "Of course you are, my dear," she said, "of course you are." And then she swept on.

—Ava Gardner

☆ ☆ ☆ ☆

One of my first times eating out in Hollywood I was at a restaurant, and there was Bette Davis! She didn't look as if she were enjoying her lunch. In fact, she was harassing the help and carrying on, and she didn't let up until the moment she left. It was quite disillusioning, because I'd thought Miss Davis was a great actress; then I found out she wasn't acting on the screen; she was just being her ornery self!

—Vera-Ellen

☆ ☆ ☆ ☆

Miriam Hopkins? She was a swine!

—Bette Davis

She's the original good time that was had by all.
                    —Bette Davis on starlet Marilyn Monroe

☆ ☆ ☆ ☆

Working with Bette Davis was one of the greatest challenges I've ever had. I meant that kindly. Bette is of a different temperament than I. She has to yell every morning. I just sat and knitted. I knitted a scarf from Hollywood to Malibu.
                                          —Joan Crawford

☆ ☆ ☆ ☆

Apparently Joan Crawford can't forget an innocent remark I made at my first Hollywood party. Back in 1947, I was a teenager looking forward to meeting movie stars, and Joan Crawford was

Myrna Loy, Bette Davis, and Constance Bennett

my favorite. At the party I said, "I'm glad to meet you, Miss Crawford. You've always been a great favorite of mine, and my mother's, too." I didn't mean to say she was older than Methuselah, but there was such an embarrassing silence I wanted to die. Since then, she's been needling me in print and at parties.

—Arlene Dahl

☆ ☆ ☆ ☆

No comment. I saw her once at her very worst. I do not condone sadism.

—Estelle Winwood on Joan Crawford

☆ ☆ ☆ ☆

I was in a play with them [Alfred Lunt and Lynn Fontanne]. Lynn was carrying on something frightful about her devotion to Alfred. Mostly for show, of course. It finally got on my nerves. One day, during a dress rehearsal, during the break, she wailed at me, wringing her hands, "Oh, where-oh-where would I be without Alfred?" I decided to tell her, for she wasn't getting any younger. I said, "You'd be right here, where I am—playing your mother."

—Estelle Winwood

☆ ☆ ☆ ☆

Estelle Winwood is not Tallulah's best friend! I am! And I've got the scars to prove it!

—Patsy Kelly

☆ ☆ ☆ ☆

Don't think I don't know who's been spreading gossip about me and my temperament out there in Hollywood, where that film was made—All About Me [All About Eve]. And after all the nice things I've said about that hag [Bette Davis]. When I get hold of her I'll tear out every hair of her mustache!

—Tallulah Bankhead

☆ ☆ ☆ ☆

[Elsa Lanchester]: Not a friendly woman, and rather daft....If she'd stayed in England, she'd have starved. She came here and made a living playing English eccentrics…and she's got barmier with the years.

—Estelle Winwood

☆ ☆ ☆ ☆

It irritated me no end that [Hermione Baddeley] and I were often mistaken for sisters or lumped together as if we were a duet. People even confused us! I would tell interviewers acidly, "No, dear, she's the fat one."…She did a play called *Diary of a Nobody.* I think she wrote it herself.

—Hermione Gingold

☆ ☆ ☆ ☆

Maureen Stapleton and I get confused for each other all the time! When she won an Oscar, I got so many congratulations, and as long as she's working, I don't mind being mistaken for her. But one time, she said to me, "If another jerk asks me if we're sisters, I'm going to say yes—and add, 'And Jean's the one who drinks!'"

—Jean Stapleton

☆ ☆ ☆ ☆

[Brigitte] Bardot was a sex symbol. Period. When she lost her looks, she lost her career, everything. Her mind went, too.

—Simone Signoret

☆ ☆ ☆ ☆

I'm not like Jane Fonda or any of these other women who say how fabulous they think it is to turn forty. I think it's a crock of shit. I'm not thrilled with it.

—Cher

☆ ☆ ☆ ☆

I went on an M-G-M junket to Africa once, and Jeanette MacDonald had her own bottled water sent from Montana, and her own sheets, and she even slept in a certain direction facing the moon every night. I said right then and there that I never wanted to be like that….

—Jane Powell

Claudette Colbert lived next door, and she'd finish a movie on Saturday—we worked Saturdays in those days—and begin wondering what she was doing Monday. I lacked that terrifying ambition.

—Irene Dunne

☆ ☆ ☆ ☆

Take Garbo. She was always sulking on a sofa in her movies. Or Marlene Dietrich, languishing in the shadows somewhere. I was never idle. There always was a broom or a vacuum cleaner in my fist, or I was at the sink, scrubbing away for dear life.

—Claudette Colbert

☆ ☆ ☆ ☆

I filmed something called *The Pleasure Seekers*...and I was sitting in the studio when I heard this real roof-shaking music coming from the dressing room of that girl—the one who has all the long blond hair and talks so soft—yes, Ann-Margret. Presently, she came out snapping her fingers and wearing a leather suit, and she hopped right on a motorcycle and roared off into the wind. I just sat back in amazement. The studio would have gone berserk if any of us had done that, back then!

—Gene Tierney

☆ ☆ ☆ ☆

I read a quote from Raquel Welch that "Carroll Baker wouldn't be sexy if she was spread-eagled naked on the cover of *Life* magazine!" I don't even know this girl; I've never done anything to her....It would never occur to me to think of another woman spread-eagled naked. It was cruel, but it was also very perverted.

—Carroll Baker

☆ ☆ ☆ ☆

I've always thought this description suited us best: Louella Parsons is a reporter trying to be a ham; Hedda Hopper is a ham trying to be a reporter.

—Hedda Hopper

Hedda Hopper had been taking potshots at me in her column for years. I finally got fed up, and around 1950 I had a live skunk shipped to her house. Later, she wrote that she'd named it Joan. A columnist always got the last word.

—Joan Bennett

☆ ☆ ☆ ☆

In Hollywood after *The Wizard of Oz,* Constance Bennett was known as the Wicked Witch of the West. A witch on wheels, if you want to be polite. And although she was very highly paid at one time, she represented the sort of actress for whom I had contempt—the type that cared more about makeup than motivation. Her face was her talent, and when it dropped, so did her career, right out of sight!

—Bette Davis

☆ ☆ ☆ ☆

I came across this old photo of Dietrich, dressed in manly attire. She was standing there in her glory, with Gary Cooper and Maurice Chevalier as her bookends. It's like what Oscar Wilde said, that nothing looks so innocent as an indiscretion....She had everyone, that one! The twist is, she preferred Chevalier to Cooper. See, Mo was supposedly impotent, at least with the ladies, whereas Coop the lady-killer supposedly had the longest handle in Hollywood. Our Marlene may have been promiscuous as all get out, but she wasn't fond of being penetrated. For one thing, she liked to be in control....

—Louise Brooks

☆ ☆ ☆ ☆

Jane Fonda's unusual for a feminist. I admire her courage, or her past courage, but she's always been very influenced by men. First by her father, then her husbands. She seems to require a strong man, either as a director—she's never had a female director—or a husband. I think she's confused. There's plenty of insecurity and pain there. That's why she's not as good at comedy; she's talented, but little sense of humor. I imagine that men have abused her, yet she seems to feel incomplete without a prominent man in her life.

—Peggy Ashcroft

Boys' night out: Maurice Chevalier, Marlene Dietrich, and Gary Cooper

I'm inclined to feel sorry for Jane Fonda. She's better at relating to groups of people than one-on-one with individual members of groups. She's cold and distant. She wants to be liked nowadays, and as she's aged, she's gotten more into herself, physically and mentally. Her passion seems to have burned itself out, and now she's sort of a beautiful...shell.

—Sandy Dennis

Mary Martin? Oh, she's all right, if you like talent.
                                                    —Ethel Merman

☆ ☆ ☆ ☆

Miss Merman is a great broad...that is, she's a great Broadway
star.
                                                    —Mary Martin

☆ ☆ ☆ ☆

I watched Barbara Stanwyck in *The Thorn Birds*. Augh! It was
painful! *I* should have played that part! She was supposed to be a
passionate older woman in love with this beautiful young priest.
She and Richard Chamberlain were completely miscast. He was
just sexless, and Stanwyck had no fire or passion, not for a man
in or out of the cloth! They made it into a *farce*.
                                                    —Bette Davis

☆ ☆ ☆ ☆

[Lillian Gish] was a sexless, silly antique.
                                                    —Louise Brooks

☆ ☆ ☆ ☆

Miss Gish in her prime made Bette Davis look like Gina
Lollobrigida!
                                                    —Joan Bennett

☆ ☆ ☆ ☆

Sophia Loren plays peasants. I play ladies.
                                                    —Gina Lollobrigida

☆ ☆ ☆ ☆

Who? I never criticize my elders.
                                    —Sophia Loren on Gina Lollobrigida

☆ ☆ ☆ ☆

Sophia Loren has a noticeable bosom. Whose is bigger, I have no
idea and could not care less. I became a star without a husband

producing my pictures, and I became a star in respectable pictures!

—Gina Lollobrigida

☆ ☆ ☆ ☆

It is a shame that Miss Lollobrigida never won the Academy Award. But she likes to play herself instead of other characters.

—Sophia Loren

☆ ☆ ☆ ☆

Lillian Gish never won an Oscar, which is shameful. For her last movie (*The Whales of August*), she should have at least been nominated. It was the final chance [in 1987] for this fine actress to win an Academy Award, an actress who was a star in *The Birth of a Nation* [in 1915]. She *must* have been disappointed, but she put a good face on it. She joked, "The only thing worse than not being nominated would have been to be nominated and then losing to Cher. *That* would have been embarrassing."

—Eva LeGallienne

☆ ☆ ☆ ☆

If you must know, I was a platinum blond bombshell before Jean Harlow was. I went to Hollywood [from England], and there I met Miss Harlow. Now, my first name is pronounced *Margo*, but twice Miss Harlow mispronounced it Margott, with a *t*. I really had nothing against her, but I must have been irritated, for I said, "It's pronounced *Margo*. The *t* is silent—as in your last name...."

—Margot Grahame

☆ ☆ ☆ ☆

They billed Vilma Banky as "the Hungarian Rhapsody." But her accent was so thick, they should have called her "Hungarian goulash." The moment talkies came in, she'd had it.

—Barbara Stanwyck

☆ ☆ ☆ ☆

Meryl Streep is so talented, she could do a remake of *The Wizard of Oz* on her own. At least all the female parts. She could act and sing Dorothy, she'd do a great Auntie Em with a Kansas twang, and she could play the Wicked Witch without needing too much makeup—she's already got the nose for it. She could even play the men, if she chose to. The only part even she couldn't touch would be Toto.

—Nancy Walker

☆ ☆ ☆ ☆

I did one film for Alfred Hitchcock [*Stage Fright*]. Jane Wyman was in it. I heard she'd only wanted to do it if she were billed above me, and she got her wish. Hitchcock didn't think much of her. She looks too much like a victim to play the heroine, and God knows she couldn't play a woman of mystery—that was *my* part. Miss Wyman looks like a mystery nobody has bothered to solve.

—Marlene Dietrich

☆ ☆ ☆ ☆

I'm funny about who I sweat with.
—Dolly Parton on why she doesn't work out with Jané Fonda

☆ ☆ ☆ ☆

When I met Shirley MacLaine, I told her right off that I don't believe in reincarnation, and we got along fine after that.
—Dolly Parton

☆ ☆ ☆ ☆

Miss [Susan] Hayward was very unkind to me on the set of *Where Love Has Gone*.

—Bette Davis

☆ ☆ ☆ ☆

She should have played my grandmother, not my mother. Then the picture might have been more interesting!
—Susan Hayward on Bette Davis

☆ ☆ ☆ ☆

Angela Lansbury hasn't a mean bone in her body. She lets the men around her do all the dirty work.

—Agnes Moorehead

At this point in her life, Angela wants to be loved. She's willing to sacrifice quality for quantity, in the number of her fans, and after so many decades in support, she's going to hang on to her leading-lady status come hell or high water. She's a wolf in sheep's clothing; in Hollywood, one has to wear camouflage in order to endure.

—Peggy Ashcroft

☆ ☆ ☆ ☆

I heard Gore Vidal wrote a novel, something thinly disguised, about me and Lana [Turner]. People tell me that if it's scandalous, I ought to sue. But why should I? If I sit tight and say nothing, no one will probably hear about it, like his other books. It's Lana who would be tempted to sue. All the energies that used to go toward her husbands now go into preserving her own legend.

—Ava Gardner

☆ ☆ ☆ ☆

We don't see each other anymore. Lana's become a recluse. No one sees her. She thinks absence will make the public's heart grow fonder. All absence does is make people think you're dead.

—Ava Gardner

☆ ☆ ☆ ☆

The heyday of the Hollywood blonde is over. Before, there was Harlow and Lana and Marilyn. Now, being blond has nothing at all to do with being sexy. There's silly, giddy Goldie Hawn or chunky Kathleen Turner, who's twice the woman—literally—that Lauren Bacall was, or Meryl Streep, who can act Polish or Australian but she sure as hell can't act blond!

—Joan Bennett

☆ ☆ ☆ ☆

Goldie Hawn is as bright as a dim bulb.

—Totie Fields

Lana Turner emoting

Kathleen Turner's okay in stills. When she talks and moves about, she reminds me of someone who works in a supermarket.
—Ann Sothern

Lauren Hutton is a magnificent model. But a model is only an imitation of the real thing.

—Lotte Lenya

☆ ☆ ☆ ☆

Suzy Parker tried to go from modeling to movies. Who else? Jean Shrimpton, Twiggy....Don't these girls ever realize it's beauty *or* talent? It takes far more effort and resources to move and act in front of the camera than to just stand still in front of it.

—Lotte Lenya

☆ ☆ ☆ ☆

I don't think some actresses can play likable. I flatter myself that my training allows me to play a bitch or else someone genuinely warm and likable, as in my new movie *Dear Heart*. Angela Lansbury's in it, too, as a cold, shrewish wife. Every movie since I can recall, she plays a bitchy personality. Not that I think she's actually bitchy off-camera, but on the screen, that's what she projects. Did you catch her in *The Manchurian Candidate*? One of the all-time wicked women! She deserved a supporting Oscar for that.

But in movies, if an actress is going to play leading roles, she has to project being likable and vulnerable. Not that she has to honestly be those things, but she has to project them, and my training allows me to project warmth even when I might be feeling distinctly icicle-ish.

—Geraldine Page

☆ ☆ ☆ ☆

What's the French word for "popsicle"? That's *her* [Capucine]. I worked with her, but when we met and shook hands, she acted as if she was nobility and I was being introduced into the royal presence.

—Anne Baxter

☆ ☆ ☆ ☆

I used to hear that William Holden was in love, at different times, with two actresses: Audrey Hepburn and Capucine. I wonder why Capucine? Was he trying to prove he runs the gamut from A to Z?

—Gloria Swanson

☆ ☆ ☆ ☆

Audrey Hepburn has exquisite manners, but my experience was that she lived and worked inside a cocoon. Very insulated. She didn't really care to venture outside it or to meet any new people. Her manners were a shade too exquisite....

—Mona Washbourne, *My Fair Lady*

☆ ☆ ☆ ☆

Roz Russell is hard as nails. They didn't cast her in all those tailored businesswoman parts in the forties for nothing. She came up the hard way, and it shows. But I'm too much of a lady to say anything nasty or repeat any rumors—I don't want to get punched in the nose!

—Ann Sheridan

☆ ☆ ☆ ☆

Maggie Smith. She's better on the stage, from a distance. On a screen, up close, she makes you want to dive for cover.

—Elsa Lanchester

☆ ☆ ☆ ☆

Elsa Lanchester is to Englishwomen what Madame Defarge is to Frenchwomen. Only, England doesn't have the guillotine...and Elsa uses her tongue to slice.

—Hermione Baddeley

☆ ☆ ☆ ☆

Poor Elsa. She left England because it already had a queen— Victoria. And she wanted to be queen of the Charles Laughton household, once he became a star, but he already had the role.

—Marlene Dietrich

☆ ☆ ☆ ☆

I asked Bette Davis if she'd ever wanted to meet the queen [of England]. She snapped at me. "What for? I am a queen." I wasn't going to argue with her!

—Natalie Wood

☆ ☆ ☆ ☆

I couldn't believe it when I heard Susan [Hayward] tried to take her own life. That is one impulse I have never understood. To want to kill someone, for a second, yes. To kill oneself, never!

—Agnes Moorehead

☆ ☆ ☆ ☆

What's with Rita Moreno? She's down to doing toothpaste commercials that misleadingly declare that she is the only actress ever to have won the Oscar, the Tony, the Emmy, the Grammy, and what-have-you. What they don't say is that it was always in the supporting category. Unlike Barbra, Liza, Julie Andrews, etc. Personally, I would never put myself in for so much potential ridicule.

—Gilda Radner

☆ ☆ ☆ ☆

Charo is a one-note song played off-key. I see her on the TV and I want to scream, "Turn her off!" She's a joke. How do they dare put her on TV so often?

—Ethel Merman

☆ ☆ ☆ ☆

Margaret Dumont had the regal bearing of a duchess. She really thought she was English. The only time I ever saw her lose her composure was when her wig slipped, fortunately not all the way off. I heard she was bald as a cue ball underneath, which may account for it.

—Marjorie Main

☆ ☆ ☆ ☆

They called Margaret Dumont the fifth Marx Brother, and apparently she didn't know whether to take it as a compliment.

Groucho always insisted she didn't understand his jokes, those somewhat benign jokes at her expense....Off the set, nobody knew a thing about her. She kept totally to herself, and I hear she never married, didn't socialize, and only showed her face when she was assigned to play one of those wonderful Mrs. Rittenhouses.

—Joan Blondell

☆ ☆ ☆ ☆

Bette Davis was known as the other Warner Brother. She loved that sobriquet because she always coveted a man's prestige, in those days. In one interview, Hedda [Hopper] inquired, "If you hadn't been an actress, what would you have wanted to be?" Bette said, "A man." Hedda loved it, but didn't use it in the published interview because she felt some people might misconstrue the answer.

—Joan Blondell

☆ ☆ ☆ ☆

Basically, Hedda Hopper used her poison pen to get back at an industry that never made a star of her in her precolumnist days, when she was struggling to survive as an actress. If she was surprised that she never really made it as an actress, she shouldn't have been. Even then, she had the face and demeanor of a ferret.

—Zasu Pitts

☆ ☆ ☆ ☆

Hedda Hopper and Louella Parsons. They were bitches!

—Elizabeth Taylor

☆ ☆ ☆ ☆

Hedda was worse than Louella. She was more vindictive. She didn't make it till later in life....

—Barbara Stanwyck

☆ ☆ ☆ ☆

Go figure those two. Hopper was homophobic, and her only child [actor William Hopper of *Perry Mason*] was homosexual.

Louella was anti-Semitic, yet she was born Jewish, then converted. They were a demented pair, and Hollywood was even more demented for allowing them so much power over people's careers and lives.

—Gale Sondergaard

☆ ☆ ☆ ☆

England has quality actresses that win all the awards but aren't exactly sex symbols. I don't get it, because all the actresses they send us from France and Italy are sex symbols rather than real talents. It's difficult to believe England has no sexy actresses and the Continent has no really talented ones. Are they all just Bardots and Lorens and Cardinals [Claudia Cardinales] over there?

—Marjorie Main

☆ ☆ ☆ ☆

Anita Ekberg is the thinking man's dunce cap. Two of them....
—Ethel Merman

☆ ☆ ☆ ☆

Ursula Undress. Isn't that her name? It should be. She's always flashing her assets all over the screen.

—Mary Astor on Ursula Andress

☆ ☆ ☆ ☆

Jayne Mansfield is to Marilyn Monroe what Richard Nixon is to Eisenhower—a crummy imitation and would-be successor.

—Vivien Leigh

☆ ☆ ☆ ☆

Before the war, actresses had personality, positive or negative. Nowadays it's mostly a busty façade, without much personality behind it. When Marilyn Monroe keeps repeating that she wants to be taken seriously as a performer, I keep asking myself, Then why does she keep accepting those idiotic roles?

—Vivien Leigh

This might be the era of the big-busted blonde, but it's also the era of the bland. I'm all for actresses whose talents don't start sagging at thirty. Someone like Bette Davis or Barbara Stanwyck will keep going long after all the Mamie Van Dorens are faded mammaries.

—Thelma Ritter

☆ ☆ ☆ ☆

The so-called love goddesses like Rita Hayworth had beauty and class. They had an unattainable quality; there was a perfection and a mystique that's vanished today. With all these peroxided blondes, there's not only no class; they seem utterly attainable.

—Lucille Ball

☆ ☆ ☆ ☆

Raquel Welch—it's no coincidence she has the same last name as a jelly. Excuse me, a jam.

—Totie Fields

☆ ☆ ☆ ☆

Marilyn was the last classic sex symbol. Who do they have now? Only Raquel Welch, who makes Marilyn look talented, and a few TV bimbo types like Suzanne Somers and Farrah Fawcett. When TV starts supplying Hollywood's sex symbols, you know that sex, interesting sex, is dead.

—Gloria Grahame

☆ ☆ ☆ ☆

Ali MacGraw is quite pretty, even beautiful at times. But she's too casual to ever rate as a sex symbol. A real sex symbol has to have or at least aspire to a degree of elegance.

—Barbara Stanwyck

☆ ☆ ☆ ☆

It must be plumb impossible to cast Lois Lane! Remember the old TV series with George Reeves? They cast someone who came off like Superman's maiden aunt. Now, in this movie with

Christopher Reeve, it's Margot Kidder, and she comes off like his goofy kid sister. Kidder has no sex appeal or pizzazz.

—Patsy Kelly

☆ ☆ ☆ ☆

Gloria Grahame is called the girl with the novocained upper lip. Donna Reed looks like the girl with the novocained face.

—Sonja Henie

☆ ☆ ☆ ☆

Clara Bow had "It." She probably caught "It" from receiving too many passes from too many football players.

—fellow redhead Susan Hayward

☆ ☆ ☆ ☆

They nicknamed me the Oomph Girl, and I loathe that nickname! Just being known by a nickname indicates that you're not thought of as a true actress....Lauren Bacall is The Look, Lizabeth Scott is The Threat, Barbara LaMarr was The Too Beautiful Girl....It's just crap! If you call an actress by her looks or a reaction, then that's all she'll ever be thought of as.

—Ann Sheridan

☆ ☆ ☆ ☆

I am the Brazilian Bombshell, but still so many people think I am Mexican. Lupe Velez is the Mexican Spitfire, and there is a Puerto Rican Pepperpot and a Venezuelan Volcano, and I don't know how many others! Not me—I am Brazilian. I born Brazilian, I die Brazilian!

—Carmen Miranda

☆ ☆ ☆ ☆

I am not the Russian Garbo. I do not know Garbo, I do not have anything in common with her. I do not like to be left alone, and I think people, and men, too, are very nice!

—Anna Sten

I'm not the new Marilyn, I'm me! Do I look like Marilyn?
> —Madonna

☆ ☆ ☆ ☆

If people want to compare me with Marilyn Monroe, let them. I can't stop people's fantasies.
> —Deborah Harry of Blondie

☆ ☆ ☆ ☆

If Roseanne Barr is the new Lucille Ball, I'm the new Garbo.
> —Nancy Walker

☆ ☆ ☆ ☆

It must be tough having a beautiful mother like Cher and being named Chastity. I guess the only thing worse would be being beautiful and being named Slut.
> —Ava Gardner

☆ ☆ ☆ ☆

I was afraid of having a daughter who looked just like Brigitte Bardot. I had nightmares about it, with my daughter being born looking just like a Bardot doll.
> —Jane Fonda, who, like Bardot, was married to
> Roger Vadim

☆ ☆ ☆ ☆

They keep comparing me to Bardot in all the magazines, but I'm not even French! I'm Swiss, and I speak German!
> —Ursula Andress

☆ ☆ ☆ ☆

The terribly unfair thing about all this is that because I also come from Sweden, I am constantly being compared to Greta Garbo, and there is no more unfair comparison than that!
> —Ingrid Bergman

I didn't know Miss [Susan] Hayward had been called "a bargain basement Bette Davis." Not until I met her and she was uncivil, and all along I had admired most of her performances. Somebody later offered that perhaps Miss Hayward actually resented the comparison to me....

—Bette Davis

☆ ☆ ☆ ☆

Only two people in Hollywood I ever wanted to meet: Garbo and Mae West. Now I've met them both, and I can go home and lie down.

—Bette Davis

☆ ☆ ☆ ☆

Hah! Joan [Crawford] must be rolling over in her grave! Long ago, they asked her if she liked any of the current crop of actresses, and she admitted to only one—she had to say *something*. So she said Faye Dunaway. Now Miss Dunaway is trashing Joan's memory in that horrendous movie (*Mommie Dearest*)!

—Bette Davis

☆ ☆ ☆ ☆

Morgan Fairchild was Faye Dunaway's stand-in in *Bonnie and Clyde*. I've met Morgan, she's a nicer person, but she's not quite...large enough. She became a *TV* star, and now she's gone and had her boobs enlarged. I don't know what possessed her. Unless it was the spirit of Jayne Mansfield.

—Nancy Walker

☆ ☆ ☆ ☆

Don't criticize people who've changed their names. Maybe the original name didn't suit them. My own name was Diana Fluck....Speaking of suggestive names, did you know Sandra Dee was Alexandra Zuck? We'd have been *fools* not to change our names.

—Diana Dors

The stupidest question I've ever been asked is whether Hermione Gingold is my real name. Now I just say, "Not really. I was born Norma Jean Baker...."

—Hermione Gingold

☆ ☆ ☆ ☆

Hollywood expressed some interest in me, but they immediately demanded to change my name. They said, "The public won't accept a star with a Jewish-sounding name." I was ready to counter with a list of Jewish movie stars, but I couldn't think of one who hadn't changed his or her name. I was appalled, and I had to question—after all, in England we had a prime minister—during Queen Victoria—his name was Disraeli....

Things are better in Hollywood now....Miss Streisand not only sounds Jewish, she looks Jewish. Most Jewish actresses do not!

—Joan Greenwood

☆ ☆ ☆ ☆

In the olden days, Jewish actresses like Kay Francis and Sylvia Sidney had to suffer in silence. But there's a lot more money to be made suffering in mink, like Joan Crawford, or suffering out loud, like Barbra Streisand. Joan played Hollywood's biggest martyrs, and she isn't even Jewish!

—Totie Fields

☆ ☆ ☆ ☆

Edith Piaf made a wonderful living out of suffering in song.

—Minnie Ripperton

☆ ☆ ☆ ☆

If you want a downer, listen to a Piaf record. If you want an upper, listen to an Ethel Merman record. It's better than drugs.

—Patsy Kelly

☆ ☆ ☆ ☆

Eartha Kitt sounds like a cat in heat.

—Ethel Merman

Who ever told Dinah Shore she could sing?

—Joan Hackett

☆ ☆ ☆ ☆

Barbra Streisand doesn't just sing; she wails. She should proudly display all her platinum records on a wailing wall. And I could support it—I could be the flying big buttress!

—Totie Fields

☆ ☆ ☆ ☆

Lena Horne opens her mouth real wide when she sings, but she's so much of a lady, just a tiny little sound comes out.

—Moms Mabley

☆ ☆ ☆ ☆

Do you know that when Whoopi Goldberg wears a dress, it's like drag....

—Mildred Natwick

☆ ☆ ☆ ☆

Bea Lillie is allegedly the funniest woman in the world, but my vote for that position goes to Martha Raye. She doesn't even have to say anything, and already she's funny.

—Marjorie Main

☆ ☆ ☆ ☆

Beatrice Lillie just published her memoirs. They're titled *Every Other Inch a Lady.* That's accurate so far as it goes, but it should have been subtitled *and Every Other Inch a Gent....*

—Patsy Kelly

☆ ☆ ☆ ☆

Today's lady comics are needlessly crude. Joan Rivers has a mouth like a manhole cover, and half of what she says is sewage. Phyllis Diller does the put-down jokes, and Moms Mabley does both these kinds of things. I can remember when Charlotte Greenwood was the toast of Broadway and then a sought-after screen comedy actress. She was a comic gem, never off-color, and a perfect lady—even while kicking up her heels sideways to touch her ears!

—Mildred Natwick

☆ ☆ ☆ ☆

Rose-Marie is the oldest female comedian. She's been onstage since Sophocles.

—Bea Lillie

☆ ☆ ☆ ☆

There was a time when I toyed with the notion of making a living doing comedy. My face can lend itself to comedy, since I'm not a classic beauty. But perhaps I wasn't homely enough. I'm certainly not aggressive or masculine enough to get up onstage and tell jokes. Few actresses are. That takes somebody like Phyllis Diller or Totie Fields.

—Geraldine Page

☆ ☆ ☆ ☆

Judy Holliday is the funniest comedic actress in pictures, and Joan Crawford is the funniest dramatic actress.

—Constance Bennett

☆ ☆ ☆ ☆

The most talented actress? Well, don't go for the obvious. Katharine Hepburn may have four Oscars, but Walter Brennan had three [supporting]. The woman's a purseful of mannerisms and gaudy affectations. Have you caught her trying to act all frilly-feminine? It's piteous. I think she's won awards for being such an independent role model, not for her acting prowess. When did she last play a villain? Or a typical female? She doesn't act, she emotes.

—Estelle Winwood

☆ ☆ ☆ ☆

I don't know if she's the most talented lady of the silver screen, but Bette Davis has taken the most risks. Some have paid off, some haven't.... Garbo might have become a great talent had she stayed with it and not darted off when the first wrinkle appeared.... I propose that for her range of roles, her career span, and her age, the most talented actress in movies was probably Shirley Temple.

—Eve Arden

☆ ☆ ☆ ☆

Ingrid Bergman has been and still is overlooked as a true talent. Was, because of her good-girl image, and she still is because of the taint of her affair with [director] Roberto Rossellini. I think she deserves another Oscar for the fine films she's done in Europe that don't get released here because of the boycott against her....
    —Anne Baxter (Bergman went on to win two more Academy Awards.)

☆ ☆ ☆ ☆

The most beautiful woman stars are Greta Garbo, Marlene Dietrich, Dolores Del Rio, and Hedy Lamarr. Not in any special order.

—Flora Robson

☆ ☆ ☆ ☆

The most beautiful female star in filmdom is Lassie. She transcends all boundaries; she's a totally sincere actress and at once a bitch and man's best friend. With gorgeous hair, yet.

—Patsy Kelly

☆ ☆ ☆ ☆

Two of the most versatile actresses I've worked with are Elizabeth Taylor and Geraldine Page [both won Oscars for *Who's Afraid of Virginia Woolf?*]. From the other side of the pond, Edith Evans is extraordinary. I'm not insulting her, but I have it from reliable sources that she's one of the few unattractive actresses who can make herself beautiful on the stage. But one of the least talented people I've worked with also happens to be British, Anne Heywood. [In *The Fox*] I played a very compelling lesbian, but I've seen two movies with Anne in them, and I swear, she wasn't very convincing as either a lesbian or as a heterosexual.

—Sandy Dennis

They asked me to star in the movie of the [lesbian-themed] play *The Killing of Sister George*. I went to see the play, and I had to say no. It's a very good play, but I told Beryl Reid, the actress who starred in it, that *she* had to star in the movie version. And she did. That role was absolutely *her.*

—Bette Davis

☆ ☆ ☆ ☆

It's hard to credit that they first offered the part of Mrs. Robinson [in *The Graduate*] to Doris Day. Happily, she turned it down. Couldn't you just see her singing an upbeat "Here's To You, Mrs. Robinson" over the credits, then trying to seduce Dustin Hoffman, then ending the affair and going home to Rock Hudson? I don't think Doris would have gotten as far with Dustin Hoffman as Rock Hudson might have; at least he'd have tried....

—Joan Hackett

☆ ☆ ☆ ☆

Raquel Welch—a moron with less on.

—Totie Fields

☆ ☆ ☆ ☆

Honey, that Totie Fields is one well-fed white woman. When that gal sits around the house, she sits around the house!

—Moms Mabley

☆ ☆ ☆ ☆

All American actresses are terrified of looking forty. What is so bad about forty? It's much better than the alternative. Someone like Joan Crawford has had two or three face-lifts, and the Gabors, they're more plastic than real. It's sad to see so much money and effort misdirected.

—Lilli Palmer

☆ ☆ ☆ ☆

I should maybe move to Europe. To France, I think. They appreciate mature women over there, and they like actresses with a little meat on their bones. If I could just lose a few pounds and talk with an accent, I could be the new Simone Signoret.

—Shelley Winters

Olivia Newton-John—Australia's gift to insomniacs. It's nothing but the blonde singing the bland.

—Minnie Ripperton

☆ ☆ ☆ ☆

Whitney Houston reminds me of that plasticky cheese that's had all the soul pasteurized out of it. She's pretty, but for a singer, pretty shouldn't matter; however, that's her main asset.

—Sandy Dennis

☆ ☆ ☆ ☆

Lauren Bacall. Yes, I worked with her. Very, very tough. A little nerve-racking for me.

Sally Fields. Very, very lucky. She escaped from television, and I don't know what she did to merit that.

Gena Rowlands. She's a good actress, but she's lucky she had a husband [John Cassavetes] whose movies she can do all the female leads in.

Oh, once I bumped into Loretta Young. Literally. I almost knocked her down, and I was so frightened. What if she'd gotten hurt and she'd sued me for ruining all that cosmetic surgery and everything? Thank goodness she didn't. She just gave me a dirty look, and it was a fierce one, yet I prize it, because you never, ever saw her give anyone a dirty look in any of her movies!

—Sandy Dennis

☆ ☆ ☆ ☆

When I was making movies, I was the only hillbilly star. I played rubes and hicks. But when I'd step out to a nightclub or a premiere, I'd get all gussied up. Now it's all topsy-turvy in Hollywood—the old glamour gals are dying off, and when you're on the town and you spot movie stars like Ali MacGraw or Julie Christie, they're dressed down in pants and denim, with their hair flying or in braids…just like when I was paid to look like a hick!

—Judy Canova

☆ ☆ ☆ ☆

It's a peculiar time [the mid-1930s] for movie entertainment. Our two biggest stars today are two blondes, different as night and

Sandy Dennis nonstop

day. Shirley Temple and Mae West. An innocent little girl whose pictures everybody wants to see and a shady lady whose pictures Shirley Temple isn't old enough to see.
—Polly Moran

☆ ☆ ☆ ☆

A swaggering, tough little slut.
—Louise Brooks speaking of eleven-year-old Shirley Temple

☆ ☆ ☆ ☆

Mae West? She's the oldest actress ever to become a sex symbol. Or should I say a lust symbol? That's fine....What's appalling is that, at 80-plus, she still believes her own publicity.
—Eve Arden

☆ ☆ ☆ ☆

I think it's sad that today's actresses feel they have to resort to advertising to make extra money. Esther Williams is selling swimwear and Marilyn Monroe sells everything under the sun. I don't mean that unkindly, but in my day, actresses had more class than that.

—ex-hat saleswoman Joan Crawford

☆ ☆ ☆ ☆

Mae West (portrait by Sue Kutosh)

I've wished I could be a stage actress, do theater on a regular basis. I've envied Sandy Dennis' career. She had a small role in one of my movies....*Splendor in the Grass*, I think. But when we met and I was going to compliment her on her Oscar for *Who's Afraid of Virginia Woolf?* she did more talking than I did. I could hardly get a word in. I think she was nervous. But she has all that nervous energy, no wonder she needs to talk all the time and talk on the stage every night too!

—Natalie Wood

☆ ☆ ☆ ☆

I think she dresses much too flashy. I also think her hair is ridiculous, and I think her behavior with Donald was very stupid. All she cares about is money, money, money. I hate that.

—Zsa Zsa Gabor on Ivana Trump

☆ ☆ ☆ ☆

She has mentioned that I was important to her, and that's very satisfying. However, a check would be better!

—Deborah Harry on being a role model to Madonna

☆ ☆ ☆ ☆

I met Zsa Zsa Gabor once at a Hollywood party. She embraced me as if we were old friends. I didn't even know her. Weeks later, she was on television saying that I had stolen the (movie) part that she played on stage (in *Forty Carats*), which was ridiculous and untrue. Anyway, I don't think we have ever been considered for the same roles.

—Liv Ullmann

☆ ☆ ☆ ☆

Sharon Stone....It's a new low for actresses when you have to wonder what's between her ears instead of her legs.

—Katharine Hepburn

☆ ☆ ☆ ☆

Take away Julie Roberts's wild mane of hair and all those teeth and those elastic lips, and what've you got? A pony!

—Joyce Haber

I met Sandra Bernhard, she was so excited....I've always heard I was sort of a mentor or something of hers, she's said so on talk shows and stuff. I guess I'll have to take her out on the town!

—Lily Tomlin

☆ ☆ ☆ ☆

All About Divas

☆ ☆ ☆ ☆

Mary Pickford was the girl every young man wanted to have—as his sister.
—Alistair Cooke

☆ ☆ ☆ ☆

She had the nerve to tell me she couldn't afford to work for a mere $10,000 a week!
—Paramount mogul Adolph Zukor on Mary Pickford

☆ ☆ ☆ ☆

It took longer to make one of Mary's contracts than it did to make one of Mary's pictures.
—Samuel Goldwyn

☆ ☆ ☆ ☆

At the studio [RKO], they called her Katharine of Arrogance. Not without reason, as I could tell you—but why bother? I really have nothing to say about Miss Hepburn which you can print.
—Estelle Winwood

I was trying the impossible, to make an artificial showcase out of an artificial star [Katharine Hepburn], and she couldn't handle it. She was hopelessly affected, babbling away like a fool and imagining it was acting.

—Broadway producer Jed Harris

☆ ☆ ☆ ☆

I don't like Katharine Hepburn. She's so holier-than-thou. She's like an old preppy with attitude.

—director John Waters

☆ ☆ ☆ ☆

Zsa Zsa The-Bore. Did I spell that right?

—Elayne Boosler

☆ ☆ ☆ ☆

Before I ever married two of the three Gabor sisters, I already knew that the words "acting" and "Gabor" are mutually exclusive terms.

—George Sanders

☆ ☆ ☆ ☆

Zsa Zsa Gabor has discovered the secret of perpetual middle age. And then some.

—John Huston

☆ ☆ ☆ ☆

Jane Fonda—from Barbarella to Stepford Wife.

—David Frost

☆ ☆ ☆ ☆

Jane Fonda's taste in husbands is downright pedestrian. First, that Chinese-looking French director [Roger Vadim], then Mr. Potato-Nose politician [Tom Hayden], now that gap-toothed cable-TV person [Ted Turner] who ruins countless films by colorizing them with arbitrary pastels. Miss Fonda always looks splendid and dresses well, but the one accessory she lacks is a good-looking or appealing husband.

—Judith Anderson

Ingrid Bergman does not look like the sort of person who would have interesting dreams. She is much too normal to be a movie star. People only *think* she is a movie star.

—Salvador Dalí

☆ ☆ ☆ ☆

Ah, yes, Mae West—a plumber's idea of Cleopatra....

—W. C. Fields

☆ ☆ ☆ ☆

I went to Mae's beach house, which she wanted redecorated if it didn't cost too much. The only sculptures she had were of herself, so I asked her if she liked painting. She said she preferred wallpaper—flocked yet! And I found out that she ordered books by the yard. The woman was virtually illiterate!

—William Haines, actor and later decorator to the stars

☆ ☆ ☆ ☆

I am not a fan of Meryl Streep. Or as I call her, Meryl Creep. I think she's creepy. Anyway, life is difficult enough without Meryl Streep movies.

—Truman Capote

☆ ☆ ☆ ☆

Dolly Parton reminds me of two big ice cream cones and a whole lot of cotton candy. She has such a sugar-coated image, and I find her repeatedly saccharine in movies. I have nothing against the gal, but I'll bet most of her fans are either hillbillies or diabetics.

—Peter Allen

☆ ☆ ☆ ☆

Take Joan Collins. She's common, she can't act, yet she's the hottest female property around these days. If that doesn't tell you something about the state of our industry today, what does?

—Stewart Granger

☆ ☆ ☆ ☆

Alla Nazimova was M-G-M's highest-paid actress in the twenties. It was common knowledge she was lesbian, and she was a Russian. Did you know that Alla was Nancy Reagan's godmother? I'm afraid Alla's claims to fame have diminished....

—George Cukor

☆ ☆ ☆ ☆

Elizabeth Taylor likes men around her. Even if it's just one and even if it's platonic. I don't think she has many girlfriends....She's a romantic, and with men around, she can have the illusion that it's romantic, but without the hassles.

—Rock Hudson

☆ ☆ ☆ ☆

I had a drag scene in Doris Day's *Glass Bottom Boat*. An elegant gown. Actually, it was more expensive than any of the ones Doris had to wear. That day that I came in fully dressed and coiffed, I was the belle of the set! Everybody went wild! Doris came over and looked me up and down and told me, "Oh, I'd never wear anything *that* feminine."

—Paul Lynde

☆ ☆ ☆ ☆

Miss [Rosalind] Russell is a very metallic personality. She wants the impossible—nothing is good enough for her....I've decided not to work with her. Life is too short, and she's too long in the tooth and ego!

—Noel Coward

☆ ☆ ☆ ☆

I was in *Bye Bye Birdie* on Broadway—played the father. I was in the film version, but they should have retitled it *Hello Ann-Margret*! They cut several of my and other actors' best scenes and shot new ones for her so she could do her teenage-sex-bombshell act. I'll admit she has charisma—on the screen. Off the screen, she is shy, or professes to be, and she speaks in such a low voice that you have to strain your ears and neck to try and hear whatever she's whispering.

—Paul Lynde

I got the part [at ten] of a herald in *Pinkie and the Fairies*. I had no idea how humble I really should have been, for the cast included Ellen Terry, Mrs. Patrick Campbell, Marie Lohr, and Lady Tree. By that time, the great Ellen Terry was nearly blind. When she first saw me in makeup, she declared that my makeup was terrible. I thought, How can she tell? She took me to her dressing room—a great honor—and I kept hoping she wouldn't mistakenly poke my eye out while she redid my makeup.

—Hermione Gingold

☆ ☆ ☆ ☆

Anita Loos wanted to put [a play] on, and I would have starred with Jeanette MacDonald....During the read-through, Mac-Donald got stony silences from the assembled company where she should have got laughs. It was a brilliant musical comedy, but she had little or no sense of humor and resented that I was getting laughs. So she withdrew, and since I wasn't a big enough name in America yet and they couldn't find a star to replace the leaden Iron Butterfly, it was all scrapped. So sad.

—Hermione Gingold

☆ ☆ ☆ ☆

Louis B. Mayer liked girls-next-door, not glamour girls. He had no taste—his taste was all in his mouth. He wouldn't let Joan Crawford keep her own name, Lucille LeSueur; said it sounded like "sewer." He lost against Greta Garbo; he thought it sounded like "garbage." All this should give you a rough idea that he was a prude with his mind in the gutter....Mayer didn't like glamorous or independent women; he preferred dumb blondes. Not that she's so dumb, but he did make a big star out of Lana Turner....

—Thelma Ritter

☆ ☆ ☆ ☆

Garbo's fans were women, not men. Women worshipped her but couldn't quite forgive her her beauty, her mystique, and so she always had to die or be killed off in each film. Unlike, say, Norma Shearer or Crawford, who were allowed to survive, but on the other hand, they had to get married and be chained down by the end of each picture.

—Susan Hayward

It's a myth about Garbo—she never decided to retire....When Garbo read Tennessee Williams's *Streetcar Named Desire*, she didn't feel anything for the Blanche character. Garbo is not scriptwise. She felt Blanche was too feminine and self-deceiving. She also hated that she lied so much. Garbo felt [Blanche] was a fool.

—Cecil Beaton

☆ ☆ ☆ ☆

Greta Garbo is a deer in the body of a woman, living resentfully in the Hollywood zoo.

—Clare Boothe Luce

☆ ☆ ☆ ☆

Like *Gone With the Wind*, Garbo is monumentally overrated. She's like a cardboard façade sprinkled with glitter, mysterious because you don't know what's behind it....Her voice is deep, she has no humor, her figure is flat, her carriage is not graceful, her feet are big, her private life is a fog....Only her face is perfect. But Garbo is smart; she quit when aging began to betray her fabulous face.

—Alfred Hitchcock

☆ ☆ ☆ ☆

I got into an elevator at M-G-M once and there in one of her famous men's hats was Garbo. I said hello, and when there was no reply, I said, "Oh, sorry, I thought you were a fellow I knew."

—Groucho Marx

☆ ☆ ☆ ☆

Raquel Welch is the rudest, most unprofessional actress I've ever had the displeasure of working with, and if I could, I would spank her from here to Aswan.

—James Mason

☆ ☆ ☆ ☆

Maggie Smith isn't so much a star as a strange voice and a bony collection of tics and mannerisms. She's doomed to a life of depicting eccentrics. The first time, she's interesting; the second time, she's quirky. After that, it grows old fast. She acts like Quentin Crisp in drag.

—James Coco

☆ ☆ ☆ ☆

[Marlene Dietrich] simply stands there, looking gorgeous—and then the effect is jarring and alienating, because she opens her mouth and the most idiotic, buttery syllables come dripping out. Clearly, everyone in the nightclub audience is there to look at her—to feast their eyes on the seeming spectacle of her having defied age. Of course, her huge mistake was to record her nightclub act.

—Quentin Crisp

☆ ☆ ☆ ☆

Diana Ross gives her all during her concerts, and does she know how to work an audience! She revels in the glory....But afterward, it was something else altogether. I was far from the biggest celebrity visiting her in her dressing room. There was a very famous actress, trying to be gracious, and the way Diana snubbed her was embarrassing for me and everyone else in the room. I've never seen anything like it, and I don't believe there's any excuse for it.

—James Coco

☆ ☆ ☆ ☆

On one occasion when Judy Garland and I embraced each other, I felt it was such a unification of two great pill repositories that it must have been a peak in pharmaceutical history. If Judy and I had married, she would have given birth to a sleeping pill instead of a child—we could have named it Barb Iturate.

—Oscar Levant

☆ ☆ ☆ ☆

The greatest performance I have ever seen was given by Tallulah Bankhead in the test she made to play Amanda Wingfield in Tennessee Williams's *Glass Menagerie*. Karl Freund photographed the test. He cried. She was dying to do that role....She had promised not to drink, but she could not keep her promise. Jack Warner said, "Errol Flynn is enough"; it cost a fortune to do a Flynn picture because he was always drunk. And thanks to Flynn, Tallulah lost the part.

—director Irving Rapper

☆ ☆ ☆ ☆

Bardot, what a cheapskate! She is known throughout France to be cheap. Once, I visit her home in St. Tropez. She had nothing in the refrigerator but water, even though her parents were staying with her. When her parents arrived, halfway during our meeting, she sent the maid out to buy a pizza—and then did not reimburse the maid, who later told me she often got stuck with the food bills but dared not complain or she would be fired. When it came time to discuss my script, she declined to read it or learn about the story or other characters. She wanted only to hear about her character. I made the character sound terrible, and she said no. I would not have let her say yes!

—director Pier Paolo Pasolini

☆ ☆ ☆ ☆

Hedy Lamarr once complained to her cameraman that he wasn't shooting her as beautifully as he'd done ten years before, on another picture. He had to be tactful, he wanted to keep his job, so he informed her, "I'm sorry, but you must remember that I was ten years younger then...."

—Jack Benny

☆ ☆ ☆ ☆

Barbra Streisand was my opening act in Las Vegas. She was multitalented from the start, but with the social instincts of a landlady. Barbra is interested in Barbra, and her only marriage that will survive is the one between her ego and her career.

—Liberace

☆ ☆ ☆ ☆

I won't go along with big-shot games. Streisand called me to read for the part of Billy Rose in *Funny Lady*. She had to do the star bit, see. So I went over to have some fun. She said, "Here, read this scene." I said, "No, let's read the whole screenplay." She read it with me, and when we finished a couple of hours later, she said, "That was great! You've got the part." I told her, "Thank you very much, but I've just done that role."

—Robert Blake

☆ ☆ ☆ ☆

She really is something, that Streisand…always got something up her skirts. I wrote a song that she claims is her favorite song ["A Sleepin' Bee"]. Which is really the song that started her career…but she doesn't sing it very well. She takes every ballad and turns it into a three-act opera. She simply cannot leave a song alone!

—Truman Capote

Barbra Streisand (portrait by Sue Kutosh)

The women have come a long way in Hollywood when the most powerful one in movies is also the least lovely.

—Lee Strasberg on Barbra Streisand

☆ ☆ ☆ ☆

Louella Parsons is stronger than Samson. He needed two columns to bring the house down. Louella can do it with one.

—Samuel Goldwyn

☆ ☆ ☆ ☆

I was teamed with Lizabeth Scott. A stunning blonde, she'd been pegged as the new Lauren Bacall. Personally, I liked her. We got along. Unlike Bacall, she never found her Bogey...and I don't think she and I had very much chemistry in any film. Nor did she generate chemistry with any of her leading men besides me, so her career stalled. Of course, there was another reason: A magazine article in the 1950s intimated that she had no chemistry with men, period. Unlike today, in those days looking fabulous wasn't enough—your image intruded even more on your private life than now.

—Robert Cummings

☆ ☆ ☆ ☆

I worked more often with Anna May Wong than anyone. She was the only Oriental star Hollywood ever produced. And even though she starred in a lot of what we might now call B-movies, she never got to kiss her leading men, because they were Caucasians. I think she did kiss the guy once, but it was some movie made in England....

—Anthony Quinn

☆ ☆ ☆ ☆

Anna May Wong had a split-level career in Hollywood. In big-budget movies she was a supporting actress, playing everyone's maid—Dietrich, Lana Turner....In small-budget movies she was the star, but they were mostly programmers, fillers like *The Lady from Chungking*. She deserved far better than Tinseltown ever offered her.

—cinematographer James Wong Howe, her cousin

Lizabeth Scott: "The Threat"

I always wanted to be Anna May Wong. She seemed so much more exotic and exciting than plain ordinary folk. But no-go. I wasn't fated to be Wong, just white.

— Paul Lynde

☆ ☆ ☆ ☆

In the 1930s and 1940s, there was Anna May Wong. Period. In the 1950s, Miyoshi Umeki won an Oscar. In the 1960s, I burst upon the scene, in *The World of Suzie Wong*, and Hollywood didn't know what to do with me. They thought I was so foreign! While it's true that my father was Chinese, from Hong Kong, my

Anna May Wong

mother is a blond English lady who lives in Florida, for goodness' sake!

—Nancy Kwan

☆ ☆ ☆ ☆

Mae West doesn't live in the real world. She has so many
illusions, we have to be very careful what we say when we're
around her now.

—Cary Grant

☆ ☆ ☆ ☆

Mae West had a screw loose, and she also had a great publicist—
herself! She always claimed she discovered Cary Grant, that he'd
never appeared on the screen before she picked him or that he'd
done only nothing little parts in nothing little pictures. Her
stories, like her wigs, varied. Here's the documented truth:
Before Miss West got her turn with him, Cary costarred with
me—in *Madame Butterfly*—and with ladies like Marlene Dietrich and Tallulah Bankhead, and none of us is exactly chopped
liver!

—Sylvia Sidney

☆ ☆ ☆ ☆

Mae West tried to bring long skirts back into fashion, but the
result was a myriad of speculation. They said her long skirts
covered a multitude of shins. Some people wondered if she had
fat legs or scars, or even a wooden leg like Sarah Bernhardt did!
Or if it was true that she was really a female impersonator and
hid her legs to keep her secret.

—Rudy Vallee

☆ ☆ ☆ ☆

I remember some magazines of the period called Jean Harlow "a
slender Mae West." Mae hated that. She generally hated all
women except her mother...and she only thought men were
good for one thing, and I don't mean drawing up contracts! Mae
hated all her rival actresses, except Marilyn, and even then she
didn't like her till she died....She used to call Dietrich "the kraut
cunt."

—George Raft

Mad about the West: Noel Coward, Mae West, and Cary Grant

I came to Hollywood too late to work with Jean Harlow, who died so tragically young. Needlessly, too, because her mother could have taken her for help in time, had the woman not been a fanatical Christian Scientist. That should have been a scandal....

It tees me off when actresses think all they have to do to become another Harlow is to bleach their hair and dress in white. They come across as cheap strumpets. She had a sensuality and a sense of humor that sparked off her sexy vibes....In *Victor/Victoria* I play a gay character, but the only drag queen in the entire movie is Lesley Ann Warren, who's made up to look like Harlow, and no comment.

—Robert Preston

☆ ☆ ☆ ☆

Greta Garbo. Well, she made a career out of a perfect profile and doing so few interviews that no way could she bore the public.

—Yul Brynner

☆ ☆ ☆ ☆

Gary Cooper and Greta Garbo are the same person. After all, have you ever seen them in a movie together?

—director Ernst Lubitsch

☆ ☆ ☆ ☆

[Garbo] had this androgynous quality. Women wanted to protect her, too, she seemed so fragile, so lovely and ethereal. Some of this was her being European, with that elegance, that aloof, almost royal quality. If she'd been American, I think the ladies in the audiences would have thought her sort of dykey. Oops!

—Gale Sondergaard

☆ ☆ ☆ ☆

There was always competition and some resentment among us American actresses, but nearly all of us looked up to and venerated such European legends as Garbo and Dietrich. It was as if they'd descended on Hollywood from Mt. Olympus. We may have admired particular American actresses like Davis or Hepburn, but we didn't feel awe for them or have that hero-worship thing toward them. Maybe you just feel more competitive or catty within your own nationality.

—Ann Sheridan

I did a movie with Garbo, and I was dumbstruck to find out that contrary to every other feminine star in town, including myself, she could do without the use of a mirror in between takes!

—Constance Bennett

☆ ☆ ☆ ☆

[Garbo] is hermaphroditic, with the cold quality of a mermaid.

—Tennessee Williams

☆ ☆ ☆ ☆

The joke around Hollywood about Garbo was, which is bigger? Her salary or her feet? I saw her in person one time, in New York, and her feet weren't anything extraordinary. Another myth dashed to pieces!

—Jack Benny

☆ ☆ ☆ ☆

Sometimes death makes a goddess. Barbara Stanwyck was no diva, she didn't have that irresistible combination of looks and personality, and her eyes were cold and small. Every female superstar has to have big or beautiful eyes. But now the media's going on as if Stanwyck was in the same league with Crawford, Hepburn, and Davis, and she wasn't. Stanwyck was never the reigning queen of any lot, and most of what she did were B-movies. What she had was staying power, and when she was done in movies, she moved on to TV, where any movie-star name seems so much bigger by contrast with TV-star names...."

—Sandy Dennis

☆ ☆ ☆ ☆

It's weird that they use the word "divas" mostly for actresses now. It's really a musical term, from grand opera. And there *are* divos...but no movie divos. Glamour in the movies is evidently limited to the female thespian....I say "divas" only in reference to great female singers. Do you realize that decades ago, Kate Smith was a diva? Which might or might not change your perspective on the use of that word!

—Peter Allen

Maria Callas is a diva. Anna Magnani is a great actress and star. My mother was a goddess. As to saints, most of them were mythical.

—Luchino Visconti

☆ ☆ ☆ ☆

It used to be that the women on the screen were larger than life. No more. Example: this new movie *The Greek Tycoon*. All about Onassis, Jackie Kennedy, and Maria Callas—fictionalized but recognizable enough to turn a profit. So it's a movie about two major, dramatic women, and yet the actresses playing them are anything but larger than life: Jackie Bisset and Marilu-some-body-or-other [Tolo]....I'm not denigrating anyone, but it is sad. They did a TV movie about gorgeous, dazzling Rita Hayworth. Who played her? Lynda Carter, for gosh sakes! There isn't a single actress in Hollywood today who could play one of the screen greats from the past, and for the life of me, I can't solve why that should be so.

—Cornel Wilde

☆ ☆ ☆ ☆

If they ever made a movie about me, there is one actress who could play me, from the purely physical point of view—Carol Kane. But I'd have to do the voice.

—Bette Davis

☆ ☆ ☆ ☆

I'm resigned to the fact that those of us who have lived our professional lives mostly on the stage—myself, Katharine Cornell, Eva LeGallienne, Edith Evans, Geraldine Page, many others as well—will not be as vivid in the memory of future generations as those who have made dozens of motion pictures or even done television....

—Helen Hayes

☆ ☆ ☆ ☆

No, I cannot accept that Lynn Fontanne is what some theatergoers call a diva. She is half of a team, and as she always acts with her husband, who knows if she alone can carry a play or if she would have as many, or half as many, loyal fans on her own? I respect Miss Fontanne, but as I understand it, a diva is an actress who brings the public into a theater or opera house—in droves, dahling—by sheer force of her unique and individual self. Not because she's playing with her husband....

—Tallulah Bankhead

☆ ☆ ☆ ☆

I know the first time I read the word "diva," in a review, I wasn't sure it didn't mean a female diver. I tend to think of water a lot, I'm from Australia....My own feeling is that the word is used inappropriately now, now that it's used only for film stars. A diva really should be a legendary stage actress. Doesn't it refer to the cult of personality? Someone like Duse, Bernhardt, or Laurette Taylor? To me, it isn't about cameras and makeup tricks, all that phony glamour of Hollywood. It's about something entirely other than looks—it's equal parts raw talent and polished personality.

—Judith Anderson

☆ ☆ ☆ ☆

I never attempted to be a film star in any way, shape, or form. I resisted it with all my might....Opera and film don't mix, and I can cite a remarkable fact which illustrates this. Only one operatic actress ever became a star in films—Geraldine Farrar. She did it in *silent* films....

—Maria Callas

☆ ☆ ☆ ☆

To be a diva, a woman has to maintain a distance from her public. First of all, there's no such thing as a TV diva, forget it. Lucy was a comic genius but not a diva. Judy Garland—a great movie star but not a diva. Not the personality of a diva. Too familiar and too accessible—and a waif—to be a diva. A diva also needs a little arrogance, or a lot, depending. I think the last divas are Barbra Streisand and Elizabeth Taylor. I doubt there'll be any younger ones. Anyone can become a movie star now; you don't need special looks or a special talent, and nowadays everyone lets everything hang out, even actresses—no distance and very little dignity.

—Robert Preston

☆ ☆ ☆ ☆

The diva thing is about strong, exciting women, and it's decided by gay men. They made a diva out of Judy Garland, also Streisand and Bette Davis, Peggy Lee, maybe. Usually it's singers. Gay men prefer strong, distinctive women, not namby-pamby ones. When I go to a party, there's always some gay men there who've showed up because they knew I was coming. Bea Arthur has the same thing. Bea and I both have that diva thing; I don't know why it is. Betty White and Rue McClanahan don't have it.

—Estelle Getty of *Golden Girls*

☆ ☆ ☆ ☆

Susan Hayward is the one actress I know that was beautiful, tough, and feminine. A total turn-on. She had the looks of a Rita Hayworth and the personality of a Bette Davis. She wasn't like Hayworth or Davis, she was her own woman, but she combined those opposite qualities. She was a gorgeous actress who you couldn't picture lowering herself to do cheesecake poses. Clearly, she was ahead of her time, which seldom pays. During the 1950s, she and Marilyn Monroe were possibly the top box-office stars, but Susan was far more highly regarded. Today she's nowhere as publicized as Marilyn, because the youth culture has taken over and the standards are shallow—skin-deep. Everything has to be beautiful but uncomplicated. And blatantly sexual. The kids just want icons—but it's idle worship. Posters, not personalities.

—Tennessee Williams

☆ ☆ ☆ ☆

Two reasons why I did not choose to go and work in Hollywood. I did not look like Miss Monroe, and I was more concerned with making good movies than choosing movies that would earn me more money, more power, more fans...and more headaches.

—Simone Signoret

I am not a diva or a legend. To be either, I think you have to be dead, or at least as old as Marlene Dietrich or Lillian Gish.

—Catherine Deneuve

☆ ☆ ☆ ☆

Joan Collins is a soap diva. It may be television and it might be formula, but *Dynasty* is a showcase for some alluring, glamorous ladies, and Joan is single-handedly restoring some star-voltage to Hollywood. She comes from a time and a place that valued personal flair and elegance.

—Jim Backus

☆ ☆ ☆ ☆

Dorothy Kilgallen had no chin, and Louella Parsons had no neck, and Hedda Hopper, she had to wear strange hats to stand out in a crowd. I don't believe most of the men columnists were failed actors, but most of the women gossips took out their frustrations on the beautiful actresses who became stars. They wrote with green ink, the lot of them!

—Ray Milland

☆ ☆ ☆ ☆

Edna Ferber was in her own way a star. The films of her novels were all major productions—I was in *So Big* early in my career, a big boost for me. But even Miss Ferber, with her great ambition, did not foist herself onto the public and the media in the same way that Jacqueline Susann or Jackie Collins have. The latest women novelists think they are stars or superstars, on the basis of their book sales! But it stands to reason—there are more people, a bigger population, so of *course* their sales are bigger than Edna Ferber's! But that doesn't make them divas, or even stars, and it never will.

—Bette Davis

☆ ☆ ☆ ☆

Grace Kelly thought that by leaving Hollywood to become the wife of a fat prince of a tiny country owned by France, she would find some greater destiny or happier status. Instead, it was the beginning of her end, and it didn't keep her from becoming an alcoholic. She wanted to get back into the movies, but it was forbidden. In the 1960s, Hitchcock made her a fantastic offer, but the Grimaldis of Monaco were still in the nineteenth-century, and Grace was stuck living inside a social refrigerator.

—Trevor Howard

☆ ☆ ☆ ☆

Princess Grace's legacy is those charming films she was in and those scandalous daughters of hers.

—Gilda Radner

☆ ☆ ☆ ☆

Princess Caroline! Who knew she was such a tramp?

—Bette Midler on Grace's elder daughter

☆ ☆ ☆ ☆

Princess Stephanie. She socializes—isn't that a genteel euphemism?—with Rob Lowe, she gets pregnant by—what?—her chauffeur or bodyguard, and—oh!—worst of all, she doesn't look at *all* like her mother!

—John Gielgud

☆ ☆ ☆ ☆

Poor Princess Grace and poor Princess Diana. Every girl's waiting for her prince to come, but why do they always have to look like Prince Rainier or Prince Charles?

—Carol Channing

☆ ☆ ☆ ☆

I wish Princess Di would move to Hollywood. She'd make a super movie star, and everyone would treat her royally, unlike that horse-faced bunch she's living among in London.

—Peter Allen

☆ ☆ ☆ ☆

It's smarter to be born a princess, if you can be. Otherwise, you have to be asked, by some not very handsome prince....Queen

Elizabeth and Queen Margaret [of Denmark] had very hand-some husbands when they were young—the husbands, I mean. Even when she's just a princess, a queen gets to choose....

—Boy George

☆ ☆ ☆ ☆

I was at a benefit rehearsal with Ethel Merman, the queen of Broadway herself. She kept wanting them to add more songs from *Gypsy*, her latest triumph. I dared to suggest another song from *my* show, *West Side Story*, and she reacted as though I were leading a palace revolution....There were others present that day, including an actress whom I won't name, but she's the only one who really stood up to the Merm, and very effectively, too. Ethel backed down immediately when this actress fixed her with her gimlet eye and said, "Don't you dare get manly with me!"

—Larry Kert

☆ ☆ ☆ ☆

Carol Channing is still wounded that whenever she's been in a Broadway musical popular enough to be made into a movie, she never gets asked—*Gentlemen Prefer Blondes* [Marilyn Monroe], *Hello, Dolly!* [Streisand], etc. But Carol has no camera tech-nique. The few chances she's had in front of a camera, she just carries on as big and bold and brassy as if she were on a stage in a cavernous theater. She will not tone it down....No wonder the drag queens love her!

—Michael Bennett

☆ ☆ ☆ ☆

Pearl Bailey has an ego that won't quit. She was in *House of Flowers*, and in it she was a madam. Well, fine, that's her persona, anyway. But in this musical, she wanted to be a madam without her girls. She didn't want any feminine competition in what she saw as her vehicle, which it wasn't. A potential hit musical, but it closed early.

—James Kirkwood, a creator of *A Chorus Line*

☆ ☆ ☆ ☆

Honey, I'm a singer from day one. Carol's a comedienne. If I have a natural gift for comedy, I can't take the praise—God gave it to

me. But I don't think too many folks outside Carol's immediate circle can claim she has a divinely inspired voice....
—Pearl Bailey comparing her and Carol Channing's turns in
Hello, Dolly!

☆ ☆ ☆ ☆

Diana Ross doesn't want to do this movie because she wants to be white.
—Ryan O'Neal about *The Bodyguard*, an interracial love story finally filmed in 1992 with Whitney Houston and Kevin Costner

☆ ☆ ☆ ☆

Gusto and packaging are everything. If you've ever doubted this, go see a Diana Ross concert in person or on video. As a voice, she's barely there, other than in the Supremes' medley when she has the backup singers. But Diana puts on a spectacle, she *is* a spectacle, and what you see is what you get. It's far and away more impressive than what you hear. She generates excitement, and that's what you pay for, the chance to feel that excited about someone or something, *sometime....*
—Raymond St. Jacques

☆ ☆ ☆ ☆

Diva-this, diva-that. It's practically a new buzzword for any female star who acts eccentric. Most divas die young; who would want to be a diva? I saw a play called *A Star Is Torn*, about diva singers, and Judy Garland, Edith Piaf, Billie Holiday—they all died before fifty! Plus others I can't recall....It boils down to what you want—an unlined, ever-youthful image like Marilyn, who died in her thirties, or to survive your youth and beauty like Jane Russell [Monroe's *Gentlemen Prefer Blondes* costar], who then goes on to become not famous, not young, not beautiful, but on the other hand, she's still here....
—Joan Hackett

☆ ☆ ☆ ☆

A genuine diva is a star with or without a man. She can even make her boyfriend or her husband, and sometimes her costar, into a celebrity, via association. Liz Taylor and Richard Burton,

Barbra Streisand with her leading men and her hairdresser-boyfriend....Have you noticed there are no more superstar couples? The last diva-divo couple was Taylor-Burton, and the last one that started off as equals, with both of them beautiful, was Vivien Leigh and Laurence Olivier. Have you seen his post-Vivien wife? Plain as plain! Could be he married her [Joan Plowright] because he grew tired of competition.

—Jill Ireland

☆ ☆ ☆ ☆

The most attractive actress never to become an international star? Virna Lisi. The least attractive star? Marie Dressler.

—Terry-Thomas

☆ ☆ ☆ ☆

I thought Hedy Lamarr was the most beautiful girl in pictures. It's a shame she doesn't get more challenging roles. I'd have thought if you looked like that, you'd get your pick of the litter.

—Linda Darnell

☆ ☆ ☆ ☆

Marilyn Monroe was not a legend in life, nor is she a legend now....I was viewing part of a television documentary about her, and one of the participants declared something to the effect that "No one ever sounded as blond as Marilyn did." What in blazes is that supposed to mean? Was he just talking to hear his head rattle? This entire Marilyn phenomenon escapes me, leaves me cold. The Bogart phenomenon I can better understand. He had a mystique, and so did his films.
Everything about Miss Monroe was and is superficial. Mere surface. She was the antithesis of a professional; her whole outlook was titillation. As when she was asked what she wore to bed and she replied, "Chanel No. 5." No actress would ever give such an impertinent, tasteless reply.

—Judith Anderson

☆ ☆ ☆ ☆

Luckily, I have not been called a "diva" in print. If I had been, I would take it as a suggestion that I should lose weight. When I think of "diva," I see someone like Elizabeth Schwarzkopf or Beverly Sills.

—Capucine

☆ ☆ ☆ ☆

One reason I slimmed down was to not fit in with the herd. I did not want to be mistaken for any other opera singer....In New York, according to a mutual acquaintance, Beverly Sills occasionally receives mail addressed to Beverly *Hills*. It must be disconcerting to be mistaken for a town!

—Maria Callas

☆ ☆ ☆ ☆

What became of Senta Berger? Back in the sixties, she was this voluptuous, elegant European beauty. Made a whole slew of films. She was all over the place. Same with several other sexy, beautiful actresses, from here and from Europe. The sixties resulted in all these sexy personalities who could have gone on to be big-time stars, but every one seems to have disappeared or died or retired....Anjanette Comer, Raquel Welch, Ursula Andress, Natalie Wood,...several others. What is it—the curse of the sixties?

—James Franciscus

☆ ☆ ☆ ☆

Interesting, this trend of famous actresses, but somewhat past their prime,...going into politics. Not in this country, but overseas. Melina Mercouri in the Greek cabinet, then running for mayor of Athens, and now Glenda Jackson in Parliament....Why don't American actresses do that?

—Sandy Dennis

☆ ☆ ☆ ☆

Melina [Mercouri] was the first actress to get deeply committed to politics. Not Jane Fonda. She had the famous family name, but Melina, who is one of my favorite costars, came first and was exiled from her own country for daring to speak out against injustice. I feel she's a bigger real-life heroine than she's been given credit for.

—Robert Morley

Karen Black was in every third movie made in Hollywood for a time. Not a beauty, but very watchable. I always felt she had a strong, raw quality, almost a drag-queen quality. The last movie I saw her in was *Come Back to the Five and Dime, Jimmy Dean, Jimmy Dean*. She played some kind of drag queen in that [a transsexual]. Now I don't see her around. Maybe stereotyping caught up with her.

—Peter Allen

☆ ☆ ☆ ☆

Hayley Mills was my favorite actress for a long time. As a kid and a teen, she had tremendous talent, and personality to spare. I can watch her movies over and over, and then suddenly, she was gone! All the more astonishing, because she was box office and she was teamed with big names. Definitely, she could have gone on to be an adult star—Natalie Wood did, and forgive me, but she had a fraction of Hayley Mills's talent. I know she up and married a man of about sixty, and she was about eighteen, which couldn't have helped her public image, but if she'd wanted to continue, I'm convinced she could have kept right on going....Must be she was forced into acting, or she got fed up with doing one film after another, and she wanted a change. But she waited too long, and although she is an actress, she's never since come close to the stardom she achieved as a juvenile, let alone surpassing it. To me, it's one of life's mysteries, and a sad little loss for me, personally. I'd love to ask her about it someday, in person.

—Joan Hackett

☆ ☆ ☆ ☆

Deborah Kerr is nice....Greer Garson is nice, and Julie Andrews and....All the English actresses are so damned nice! Except Hayley Mills. Thank God.

—John Huston

☆ ☆ ☆ ☆

I believe it's Louis B. Mayer or Samuel Goldwyn who described Greer Garson as a perfect lady. Or was that Deborah Kerr? But a perfect lady is hardly an exciting star, or an enduring one. It is the bitches who last the longest, because they are the most intriguing!

—Fernando Lamas

☆ ☆ ☆ ☆

I did some entertaining, fun, not too memorable pictures with Paula Prentiss. She was the greatest thing since sliced bread. Brilliant comedienne. Sexy, too. You know what killed her career? Her marriage [to actor-director Richard Benjamin]. I have no idea if it was entirely her decision, but she let their marriage and his career come first, before her career. She was a star, he wasn't, and he doesn't have star quality. But that's what she did.

—Jim Hutton

☆ ☆ ☆ ☆

Jean Arthur was one of the leading stars of the 1930s, an American original....She loathed every minute of it. I never knew an actress who so dreaded the camera or going out before the cast and crew on a soundstage. Cinephiles comment on how brief her career was; I'm surprised she let it go on for as long as it did! That poor girl suffered for her art! In front of the camera, she was bubbling and radiant, but when it wasn't running, she was in torment....Paranoid, too. Not clinically paranoid but suspicious that nobody was on her side. She never really relaxed into a camaraderie with any of us....I hope she's happy now, a recluse by the seashore. I couldn't imagine living that way, after the bright lights of celebrity life.

—Cary Grant

☆ ☆ ☆ ☆

Fellow actor made a picture with Ginger [Rogers], came to me and said, "She's not very easy to know, is she?" I said, "Not if you're lucky, old man."

—Cary Grant

☆ ☆ ☆ ☆

Not that she [Ginger Rogers] was standoffish. Not to me, not much. Condescending, yes. It was the girls with smaller roles, with token lines of dialogue or no lines at all, that she treated like mosquitoes.

—Eve Arden

☆ ☆ ☆ ☆

Betty Hutton was the most self-destructive star of them all. I knew her, worked with her, laughed with her. She had too much energy, far too much energy. Hyperkinetic [sic]....The higher she went, the more certain she was that she alone knew how to manage her career, and she craved more and more say-so....Now look at her: Hollywood's biggest tragedy. The higher they go,...

—Billy De Wolfe

☆ ☆ ☆ ☆

There are different degrees of masochism. When Betty Hutton replaced Judy Garland in *Annie Get Your Gun*, I remember everyone agreeing that Judy was through in this town. The drugs and the suicidal despair had taken over. This was, oh, about 1950. Hutton was on top of the world. A couple of years later, Hutton was washed up, on an irreversible downward spiral. Judy came back big, in *A Star Is Born* and eventually in live performance. Of course she died far too young, but her career and stardom easily eclipsed Betty Hutton's.

—Fred Astaire

☆ ☆ ☆ ☆

Liv Ullmann is an undeniable talent, but what a brooding presence! Seems as if all the ladies out of Scandinavia have to make an effort to be happy.

—Vincent Price

☆ ☆ ☆ ☆

Celia Johnson, my would-be lover in *Brief Encounter*, was made into a star by Noel Coward. She could have carried on and been our preeminent film star, but she was forever interrupting her career to have children. She was what one could call a family woman.

—Trevor Howard

Audrey Hepburn walked out on her thriving career in the late sixties, terminated it, for her second husband. An Italian—a philandering Italian. He left her for a younger woman. You see?
—Romy Schneider

☆ ☆ ☆ ☆

If it hadn't been for costarring with Spencer Tracy all those times, Katharine Hepburn would have spent the second half of her career playing nothing but spinsters.
—Edith Evans

☆ ☆ ☆ ☆

Why is it the wildest personal rumors accrue to the most innocuous actresses? There's that rumor that June Allyson is an alleged nymphomaniac and the one that Julie Andrews is tougher than a five-star general.
—Rock Hudson

☆ ☆ ☆ ☆

I'm not a Julie Andrews fan, no. I'm a diabetic.
—David Janssen

☆ ☆ ☆ ☆

I'm nutty for women with funny voices. June Allyson sounds like she swallowed a frog, and Lauren Bacall—gravel, baby, gravel!
—Zero Mostel

☆ ☆ ☆ ☆

Claire Bloom is one of the best actresses working today. If she had done nothing more than *Limelight* with Charlie Chaplin, her place would be assured. But Miss Bloom must not be an active self-promoter. She is talented and beautiful but very low-profile. Could she be the one actress who is really telling the truth when she says in interviews that she is shy?
—Lilli Palmer

Claire Bloom is absolutely wonderful. Except in comedy, where she's horrible.

—George Cukor

☆ ☆ ☆ ☆

Beats me why Eleanor Parker was through by the time she was forty. She had everything—looks, talent, character, Oscar nominations. It's one of those situations where the only logical answer to the question Why didn't she become a bigger star? must be that she refused to sleep with some mogul or top producer. Nothing else would make sense.

—Stephen Boyd

☆ ☆ ☆ ☆

There's only one actress I can think of who acts as if she couldn't care less about being a movie star—Julie Christie. So, either she doesn't, or she's an even better actress than we think.

—Peter Finch

☆ ☆ ☆ ☆

Tatum O'Neal....The comparisons to Shirley Temple are disgraceful! She acts like a hoyden [on the screen], and it's encouraged. Producers with very immature tastes derive pleasure from watching child actresses and actresses in their seventies and above acting like tarts...and then to give her an Academy Award [for *Paper Moon*] on top of it!

—Joan Bennett

☆ ☆ ☆ ☆

In the past, you heard about actresses in their thirties taking to the bottle because their careers or their marriages were on the wane. Now a girl's washed up at fifteen, and it's headlines about teen actresses like Linda Blair and Drew Barrymore checking into the Betty Ford Clinic to conquer their boozing or their drug addiction. By the ripe old age of twenty, hopefully they've become sober, wise old souls.

—Bert Convy

I don't have it in for Brooke Shields or *Time* magazine, although I always held that it's an overestimated rag, but appearing on the cover of *Time is* a type of benchmark for some VIPs, only doesn't Brooke Shields appearing on the cover of *Time* sort of diminish how meaningful that particular distinction really is?

—Peter Allen

☆ ☆ ☆ ☆

Hollywood is so ironic....The most powerful woman ever in motion pictures was Mary Pickford, who rarely didn't portray a little girl. "Little Mary," as she was called, cofounded United Artists, and her home, Pickfair, was Hollywood's Buckingham Palace. Now Pickfair has been torn down by Pia Zadora, one of Hollywood's most peripheral actresses or singers or....I mean, Pia Zadora! *Mary Pickford....*

—director Derek Jarman

☆ ☆ ☆ ☆

I briefly considered Streisand as a Jewish nun. But I'm personally turned off her. Until recently, she was anything but pro-gay, despite the fact that all her male fans are gay—I mean, straight men can't stand her, except as a singer—and her only child (Jason Gould) is reportedly and allegedly a gay man who has optioned a gay love story and who took part in a wedding ceremony with his male life partner. I mean, I know she's wrapped up in herself, but how could she be so dense?

—"Sister Act" director Emile Ardolino

☆ ☆ ☆ ☆

We had personalities then....Carmen Miranda was colorful in black-and-white!

—Betty Grable

☆ ☆ ☆ ☆

Who, Streisand? The face, that's a matter of opinion. But the voice is beautiful, the ego rather ugly. She'll never be nominated for another Oscar—she's alienated too many people in this town.

—Lee Remick

Carmen Miranda: Colorful in black-and-white

Tinseltown loves a buck, but they're terribly impressed by talent. That's why they tolerate Vanessa Redgrave, who's a Trotskyite Marxist, anti-Israel, and the first famous unwed mother not to marry her child's father. She's also obnoxious, strident, and difficult to work with, and I should know.
                    —Anthony Perkins of *Murder on the Orient Express*

Vanessa Redgrave: Them thar shoulders

I've seen *Roseanne*. John Goodman is fine...(but) she's a pig.
—Larry "Dallas" Hagman

☆ ☆ ☆ ☆

So many Hollywood people were endorsing Clinton, you wanted to say, "Someone should hang back; someone has to be in the business after Barbra (Streisand) sings."
—Robin Williams

☆ ☆ ☆ ☆

Two of Britain's five richest women live in Los Angeles. Angela Lansbury and Jackie Collins. People find this rather surprising in England, however in California people can't quite understand why any rich non-royal would still live in England!
—John Schlesinger

☆ ☆ ☆ ☆

Ex-Husbands and -Wives

☆ ☆ ☆ ☆

Desi [Arnaz] is a loser. A gambler, an alcoholic, a skirt-chaser...a financially smart man but self-destructive. He's just a loser.

—Lucille Ball

Lucy isn't a redhead for no reason. She has a big comic talent, but she also has a big, not very funny temper. Not a temperament but a *temper*. Her tongue is a lethal weapon. She can be very cruel when she wants to be.

—Desi Arnaz

☆ ☆ ☆ ☆

Joan Collins is a commodity who would sell her own bowel movement.

—Anthony Newley

☆ ☆ ☆ ☆

Yes, Vanessa Redgrave is controversial. Her enemies hate her, and her friends dislike her. A great actress. Not a great thinker, though. Me, I'm leftist; her, she's often just plain lunatic!

—director Tony Richardson

109

The first time I saw George Burns onstage I could see that he had what it takes to become a big star: Gracie Allen.

—Bob Hope

☆ ☆ ☆ ☆

Far more versatile than people remember, but she chose to hide her bushel under Charles Laughton's great big light.

—Hermione Gingold on Elsa Lanchester

☆ ☆ ☆ ☆

Charles Laughton was not handsome. But I resented it when people called me "the bride of Frankenstein" behind my back. For Charles did *not* appear in my most famous film, *The Bride of Frankenstein.*

—Elsa Lanchester

☆ ☆ ☆ ☆

Janet Leigh was years ago! Nowadays I wouldn't be caught dead married to a woman old enough to be my wife!

—Tony Curtis

☆ ☆ ☆ ☆

My marriage to Angela Lansbury lasted several months. It's always in my résumé, never in hers. She chooses to forget that I was her first. Husband, that is.

—actor Richard Cromwell

☆ ☆ ☆ ☆

I always knew he'd end up in bed with a boy!

—Ava Gardner, after ex-husband Frank Sinatra wed Mia Farrow

☆ ☆ ☆ ☆

Of course I married Artie Shaw. Everybody married Artie Shaw!

—Ava Gardner (so did Lana Turner)

Ava and Artie: Gardner and Shaw

With Nick Arnstein, I was miserably happy. With Billy Rose, I was happily miserable.

—Fanny Brice

☆ ☆ ☆ ☆

Jackie married Jack Kennedy for love, I suppose, but didn't get it. She married the Greek [Onassis] for money and got it. You tell me which was the more successful marriage....

—Gabrielle "Coco" Chanel

☆ ☆ ☆ ☆

Ernest Borgnine must be *muy macho.* I think that's why he married Katy Jurado and Ethel Merman—pretty macho women. Think of it—Borgnine and the Merm: that's a lot of testosterone!

—Jacqueline Susann

☆ ☆ ☆ ☆

Gary Merrill was a macho man, but none of my four husbands was man enough to become Mr. Bette Davis!

—Bette Davis

☆ ☆ ☆ ☆

William Wyler, the great director, wanted to marry me. I truly was foolish not to! I understand that Jewish husbands usually stay the course, and I might have had one long, happy marriage instead of four relatively short ones. My friend Joan Blondell calls my four husbands the "four skins." She married a Jewish man [producer Mike Todd]...but he left her for Elizabeth Taylor....When it comes to husbands, there really are no guarantees, except headaches along the way. Brother!

—Bette Davis

☆ ☆ ☆ ☆

Richard [Burton] is so discriminating, he won't see a play with anybody in it but himself.

—Elizabeth Taylor

Yes, Elizabeth and I have been previously bound in matrimony. However, that was a dress rehearsal for this—you know what they say about the second time around....

—Richard Burton

☆ ☆ ☆ ☆

R.J. [Robert Wagner] and I are settling down for good. The first marriage was just a rehearsal for the second one. Neither of us will ever marry again....

—Natalie Wood

☆ ☆ ☆ ☆

I married three actresses. All the world's a stage, and that includes the bedroom....

—Laurence Olivier, who wed Jill Esmond, Vivien Leigh, and Joan Plowright

☆ ☆ ☆ ☆

When I walked into that room and found Mick [Jagger] and David [Bowie] together, I felt absolutely dead certain that they'd been screwing. It was so obvious, in fact, that I never even considered the possibility that they hadn't been screwing....I didn't have to look around for open jars of K-Y Jelly.

—Angela Bowie

☆ ☆ ☆ ☆

Rex Harrison had a mistress [actress Kay Kendall]. I would have been upset, except that I had a lover. He took it a step further and asked me to grant him a divorce so he could marry the young lady—or young woman. I thought he was insane until he told me that Kay had only a year or two to live. Then I of course gave him the divorce. People were astonished, but it was merely civilized behavior. The idea was that after Miss Kendall passed away, Rex and I would remarry. He fully expected that to happen, but he didn't count on my falling in love with *my* lover [actor Carlos Thompson]....
Instead, I married Carlos, who is far more of a star in my life than Rex Harrison ever was.

—Lilli Palmer

What *made* him, originally, was starring in gossip. Wives, lovers, the Carole Landis suicide....He genuinely hated all that scandalous publicity. On the other hand, he was so privately grateful to finally become a star.

—Rachel Roberts on Rex Harrison

☆ ☆ ☆ ☆

"Sexy Rexy"...I think they came up with that nickname because gossips love things that rhyme. Brief, clever, witty, catchy. "Sexy Rexy." He's sexual, or was. But not in an obvious way. He needed quite a bit of stimulation....

—Rachel Roberts

☆ ☆ ☆ ☆

Rex cannot be pleased. Servants have got slapped with his tongue or hand. Eventually, his servants and wives leave him. Rex is one of those what thinks living well is the best revenge. It may be, but the revenge is taken out on his nearest and his dearest.

—Rachel Roberts

☆ ☆ ☆ ☆

Fred Astaire did not have a huge feud with Ginger Rogers. The feud was between Rogers and Fred's wife, a tiny, rich woman who was very much in charge. She wouldn't let Fred and Ginger dance together offscreen. She was jealous of Ginger; maybe she imagined Ginger wanted to have an affair with Fred, which I'm sure she didn't—unlike me, Ginger liked handsome men. As for Fred, I honestly don't think he was anything other than basically asexual.

—Ava Gardner

☆ ☆ ☆ ☆

I married late; my husband [actor Stringer Davis] married late. We are the best of friends. He told me he had a crush on John Gielgud, and I respect that. We two are loving companions—no less and no more.

—Margaret Rutherford

I did have one homosexual husband. At least. Guthrie McClintic. He was an extremely famous Broadway producer who loved his fellow man—often. I wasn't the only actress he married. He married Katharine Cornell. But it was different for her than me—like her husband, she was attracted to her own kind. You know: Birds of a feather fornicate together.

—Estelle Winwood

☆ ☆ ☆ ☆

I was married to the brother of St. Nick. You know that picture *Miracle on 44th [34th] Street.* The one who played Santa Claus [Edmund Gwenn]—I forget his name. Anyway, his brother— that's who I was married to. I forget his name as well....

—Estelle Winwood

☆ ☆ ☆ ☆

Gable's first two wives were older women and decidedly not beauties. But rich....He may have been, initially, a gigolo at heart. That may be why his persona was treating women badly, which was not unacceptable then. Clark used his first wives to work his way up....He may have been a divine sex symbol, but he wasn't a prize husband.

—Eve Arden

☆ ☆ ☆ ☆

If Clark had one inch less, he'd be the "queen of Hollywood" instead of "the king."

—Carole Lombard, Gable's third wife

☆ ☆ ☆ ☆

Bogart fell in love with the character Bacall played in *To Have and Have Not,* so she had to keep playing it for the rest of her life.

—director Howard Hawks

☆ ☆ ☆ ☆

I knew John Lennon a little bit, and I liked him a lot. He was very intelligent. He was a sensitive, good-hearted person. I couldn't stand *her* [Yoko Ono]. The Jap. She was always paranoid. The most unpleasant person that ever was, in my opinion. She's a bore.

—Truman Capote

☆ ☆ ☆ ☆

I felt extremely sorry for his [Johnny Carson's] second wife, Joanne. She was very good to him. She did a tremendous amount for Johnny. I don't think Johnny would have survived or have had remotely the career he's had if it hadn't been for her. But he was mean as hell to her. And they lived right next door to me, for years. He would holler and get terribly angry, and she would take refuge in my apartment. She would hide, and Johnny would come pounding on my door, shouting, "I know she's in there." And I would just maintain a dead silence.

—Truman Capote

☆ ☆ ☆ ☆

I married Vincent Price very late in both our lives. It was chiefly because, even if Vincent can be a bit moody or frightening at times, loneliness is even more frightful. Without a husband, even an actress doesn't get invited out much. In Hollywood, a woman without a set of masculine appendages attached to her name doesn't rate, socially. Here feminism is a foreign concept— something imported from New York or elsewhere.

—Coral Browne

☆ ☆ ☆ ☆

Never marry a director. He'll want to direct you at home, too. It happened to me with Roberto Rossellini, and Paulette Goddard says the same of Charlie Chaplin.

—Ingrid Bergman

☆ ☆ ☆ ☆

I tried hard to make my marriage [to actor Mel Ferrer] work. I discovered that actors are always competing. The men, anyhow. So I cut back on my film schedule, did fewer movies, was with him more often. It still didn't work out, because even if I worked less, I couldn't make myself a smaller star—small enough to please him....

—Audrey Hepburn

When Fernando [Lamas] proposed to me, he said, "Let me take you away from all this." And I said, "Away from all what? I'm a movie star!"

—Esther Williams

☆ ☆ ☆ ☆

Anne Bancroft married Mel Brooks. Shirley Jones married Marty Ingels. What can these people possibly have in common? Are those marriages or stunts? I can't figure it out.

—Lucille Ball, who also married a comedian
[Gary Morton]

☆ ☆ ☆ ☆

Have you noticed how many singers and actors marry models? It's those shallow men who want a pretty something without much brains or talent, not a real woman, not competition. In show biz, you can judge a man by his wife. Most actors pick wives the way most American men pick automobiles....John Travolta, Richard Gere, Billy Joel, etc. Warren Beatty, if he ever does marry, will choose a model or some sort of nonstar. Those men want trophies, not partners, and certainly not equals.

—Glenda Jackson, MP (Member of Parliament)

☆ ☆ ☆ ☆

Richard Gere and Cindy Crawford—he's elastic and she's plastic.

—Sandra Bernhard

☆ ☆ ☆ ☆

Madonna and Sean Penn—beauty and the beast, but guess which one?

—Joan Rivers

☆ ☆ ☆ ☆

Joan Crawford's first marriage was very shrewd on her part. She married for social position in Hollywood. It didn't matter a bit that it was Douglas Fairbanks Jr. Joan had set her sights on Mary Pickford as an in-law; she married into Pickfair. It just happened that Junior was the son of Douglas Fairbanks Sr. and the stepson of Mary Pickford. That put Joan on the map, and she more than took it from there!

—Charles "Buddy" Rogers, Pickford's last husband

☆ ☆ ☆ ☆

Joan Crawford thought about marrying Clark Gable and even considered me for a while. But I don't think either Clark or I would have relished playing a supporting part in Miss Crawford's private life....My advice to most any man in this business is, don't marry an actress, and I know whereof I speak.

—Henry Fonda

☆ ☆ ☆ ☆

In an agent's office, I overheard an actor say Margaret Sullavan was having an affair with the producer Jed Harris....I'd lean against the fence and I'd stare up at our apartment with the lighted windows on the second floor. More nights than I care to remember I'd stand there and cry....I couldn't believe my wife and that son of a bitch were in bed together. But I knew they were. And that just destroyed me.

—Henry Fonda

☆ ☆ ☆ ☆

I left [husband Burt Reynolds] the day he threw me against our fireplace and cracked my skull.

—Judy Carne

☆ ☆ ☆ ☆

Orson Welles sometimes gave me cause to think that he married me so he could direct me. Off the set and, in particular, on it. If the film we did (*The Lady from Shanghai*) had been more successful with the public, our marriage might have lasted longer.

—Rita Hayworth

☆ ☆ ☆ ☆

Lana Turner and I had some good times together. Especially before the nuptials.

—Lex Barker

Lex Barker was very handsome....Just plain handsome.
—Lana Turner

☆ ☆ ☆ ☆

Lana Turner's not an outstanding actress, but a man is better off with a woman who can't lie too well. I'd be uncomfortable married to, say, Katharine Cornell.
—Lex Barker

☆ ☆ ☆ ☆

Simone [Signoret] is a very patient woman. She has to be to stay married to me. I am so happy that she has never thrown me out. Very long ago, Edith Piaf threw me out, and for me it was a great tragedy, although I was not married to her.
—Yves Montand

☆ ☆ ☆ ☆

You never really know about chemistry. I directed Monroe and Montand in *Let's Make Love*, which they proceeded to do. Miss Signoret was accompanying her husband [in L.A.], but right under her nose he had an affair with Marilyn. They were intoxicated with each other. But on the screen? Marilyn. Yves. *Nothing!*
—George Cukor

☆ ☆ ☆ ☆

Helen Hayes had the extreme bad taste to mention one of my two ex-husbands, both of them experiences too dreadful to discuss. She had no provocation for mentioning him. So now she's on my enemies list.
—Judith Anderson

☆ ☆ ☆ ☆

I am married to a fine actor named Rip Torn....The mail carriers are used to our mailbox, which reads *Torn Page*.
—Geraldine Page

☆ ☆ ☆ ☆

Being married to Arlene Dahl was very nice, at nighttime. But in the daytime, it was like being married to Elizabeth Arden. That is where she spent most of her time. If you asked her which was more important to her, her home life or her career, she would have to tell you the truth: her face!

—Fernando Lamas

☆ ☆ ☆ ☆

Not many women can say they voted for their ex-husband. Even fewer would want to.

—Jane Wyman on Ronald Reagan

☆ ☆ ☆ ☆

Ida [Lupino] is a wonderful wife and a wonderful director, and she never gets the two mixed up. In a marriage, the husband has to be the producer and the director. The wife gets to always be the leading lady.

—Howard Duff

☆ ☆ ☆ ☆

Ida Lupino is a first-rate actress and director. But our marriage was stormy. She wasn't as easygoing or lazy as I basically am. She tried awful hard, but we were a competitive pair, and competition might be fun at first, but when you're older, you want to give it a rest.

—Howard Duff

☆ ☆ ☆ ☆

Living with Jane [Fonda] was difficult in the beginning....She had so many—how do you say?—bachelor habits. Too much organization. Time is her enemy. She cannot relax. Always there is something to do—the work, the appointment, the telephone call. She cannot say, "Oh, well, I'll do it tomorrow." This is her weakness.

—Roger Vadim

☆ ☆ ☆ ☆

My mother liked Brigitte [Bardot] very much, but she always said, "I feel sorry for her....She'll never learn to grow up. I think she'll always be a child. To be happy you must know how to love. She has a passion for love but doesn't know how *to* love."

—Roger Vadim

☆ ☆ ☆ ☆

To outsiders, [Catherine Deneuve] appeared to be balanced and self-controlled in all circumstances. Nevertheless, she did have moments of extreme irritability, and she gave in to sudden fits of jealousy which were rarely justified.

—Roger Vadim

☆ ☆ ☆ ☆

I do not live my life in a conventional way. I was legally married once, to a photographer [Englishman David Bailey]. We had no children. I have a child by Marcello Mastroianni and another by Roger Vadim. I did not plan it like that, it just happened, and I do not give explanations or apologies.

—Catherine Deneuve

☆ ☆ ☆ ☆

Brigitte Bardot asked me to marry her. I don't know if she was joking, but I said no. I did not explain that I couldn't marry an actress who could never be faithful to me. Or at least try. Like I would at least try, for the first year or two.

—Stephen Boyd

☆ ☆ ☆ ☆

Simone [Signoret] is very talented for living in the present, in reality and not a romantic past. She is a happy realist, which is rare. The title of her book gives her philosophy—*Nostalgia Isn't What It Used to Be.*

—Yves Montand

☆ ☆ ☆ ☆

I never daydream about him, no....When I listen to his records, I feel free to criticize his voice.

—Signoret on Montand

☆ ☆ ☆ ☆

I was married to Britt Eklund. I do not advise marriage to a blond actress....

—Peter Sellers

☆ ☆ ☆ ☆

Some famous wit said that my wife, Esther Williams, is a star only when she is wet. *He* is all wet! Another rumor is that I made Esther give up her career when we got married. That is a lie! She was already washed up when we got married.

—Fernando Lamas

☆ ☆ ☆ ☆

Shirley Jones should have become a bigger star than she did. She can do more than play a goody-goody, but she had the bad luck to be a good-looking blonde who is not a sex symbol. I admit that her stardom, when she was in *Oklahoma*, was very attractive to me. I wanted to be a movie star, myself. I married Shirley, and with time I found out that in this life you almost never get what you want, or you end up not wanting what you got. It's too bad.

—Jack Cassidy

☆ ☆ ☆ ☆

My marriage to Sheila began to end when she wouldn't accommodate my drinking and began concentrating on her own career. I think the wife I should have had would be a stay-at-home alcoholic. Someone like Dixie Lee, who was married to Bing Crosby. I'd have been kinder to her than Crosby was, and she'd have been more sympathetic to me....

—Gordon MacRae

☆ ☆ ☆ ☆

Bela Lugosi is no gentleman. We made several pictures together, and he never liked me, I assume because I'm English and have a better command of the language and receive better offers....He used to admit that he beat his wives and once even bragged about it. He said that he suspicioned his then-wife of having an affair and that he not only beat her unconscious, but he would strangle her if he found out it were true. I was appalled and made it known. He laughed that demonic cackle of his and shrugged, "Ah, the English!"

—Boris Karloff

☆ ☆ ☆ ☆

Bela Lugosi: A stifling husband

Being married to Dyan Cannon was no picnic, but we had a child together, my only child. It seems that each new marriage is more difficult to survive than the last one. I'm rather a fool for punishment—I keep going back for more, don't ask me why.

—Cary Grant

☆ ☆ ☆ ☆

I know they nicknamed us "Cash and Cary," but I never asked [Woolworth heiress] Barbara Hutton for a penny. I never married a woman for money, that's the God's truth. I may not have married for very sound reasons, but money was the least of them.

—Cary Grant

☆ ☆ ☆ ☆

I fell in love with Cary Grant....He did not reciprocate the emotion, and that disappointed me. Then I spoke with one of his ex-wives, whom I prefer not to name, and she revealed that he is not prone to falling in love with, let us say, actresses....Cary and I became good friends. Not close friends, because he doesn't let you come too close. If we had gotten married, I doubt he would have let me get too close....It is better to have a crush on Cary Grant than to have him for a husband. A crush allows you to keep your fantasies....

—Ingrid Bergman

☆ ☆ ☆ ☆

Being married to Olivia Hussey isn't exactly a Romeo and Juliet thing. [Hussey costarred in *Romeo and Juliet*]. I'm no Romeo. Part of the time, I'm more interested in my gun collection than my wife, even though I do love her and I don't love my weapons.

—Dean Paul Martin

☆ ☆ ☆ ☆

What's it like being married to Dorothy Hamill? Sometimes it's like skating on thin ice.

—Dean Paul Martin

☆ ☆ ☆ ☆

"Cash and Cary:" Barbara Hutton and Cary Grant

Ali MacGraw is a good wife for me. We're both actors, but neither of us is a great, big, fat talent, and she's not all wild-eyed about her career, which suits me fine.

—Steve McQueen

☆ ☆ ☆ ☆

We started as husband and wife, but it ended like brother and sister.

—Elizabeth Taylor on Michael Wilding

☆ ☆ ☆ ☆

Ours was not a passionate marriage; it was a wonderful friendship, and that is as good a reason as any to get married.

—Margaret Leighton on Michael Wilding

☆ ☆ ☆ ☆

Laurence Harvey married me as much for his career as for my willingness to subordinate myself and be his nanny....I was flattered to have a younger man show interest in me. What can I say? I was a bit foolish.

—Margaret Leighton

☆ ☆ ☆ ☆

I will always feel married to Mr. Olivier, in one way or another.

—Vivien Leigh on her ex, Laurence Olivier

☆ ☆ ☆ ☆

The irony is that Larry's first wife [actress Jill Esmond] was a reputed lesbian, and they did have offspring. Larry and Vivien, who was an actress but heterosexual, did not. Then he married one more actress, and they have offspring, yet I understand she is heterosexual....Is Larry heterosexual? I'm the wrong chap to ask.

—Peter Finch

☆ ☆ ☆ ☆

Mia Farrow's taste in men is nothing if not eclectic. The one common thread uniting her husbands and men is show business. Sinatra, then [André] Previn, that cinematographer [Sven Nyquist], now Woody Allen. Not a good-looker among them! I think she wants to mother them; some actresses are more the mothering type than the seductress or mistress type....Mia looks like a shy little orphan, but she wants to be Mother Courage, and I think she is!

—John Cassavetes

☆ ☆ ☆ ☆

I hold that actresses like Vanessa Redgrave and Farrah Fawcett are giving our profession a bad name, having children out of wedlock. It's more shocking in Miss Fawcett's case, for she had a

Mamma Mia: Farrow and John Cassavetes

husband [Lee Majors, before longtime companion Ryan O'Neal] and they didn't have even one child....

—Irene Dunne

☆ ☆ ☆ ☆

Life can be depressing enough without having a comedian for a husband. I'm not expressing myself right: What I'm saying is, being Gene Wilder's wife makes my life a little less realistic. Comedy is grounded in reality, but it can't be tied to it. What I'm really trying to say is, I wouldn't want to be married to Clint Eastwood.

—Gilda Radner

☆ ☆ ☆ ☆

Sean [Penn] tried to be a good husband. He just tried too hard....

—Madonna

☆ ☆ ☆ ☆

Shelley Winters has a fondness for Italian men. She married me and Anthony Franciosa. But she doesn't like Italy enough, and to me it was more important to be at home in Italy than to be in America with her. Mamma Italia comes first.

—Vittorio Gassman

☆ ☆ ☆ ☆

I did not want to be known as Kate Smith.
    —Katharine Hepburn, replying to why she divorced Ludlow Ogden Smith

☆ ☆ ☆ ☆

I was married to Maria Montez until she died prematurely in a freak accident. In her career, she was very aggressive, while at home she wanted me to be the master. When we had guests....Maria had many fantasies; she was always trying to make her dreams come true. She was exceptionally vain, but childlike in other ways. She did have a hot temper, but she also

Maria Montez (portrait by Sue Kutosh)

sacrificed in her career to make our marriage possible to continue.

—Jean-Pierre Aumont

☆ ☆ ☆ ☆

Ginger Rogers was married to her career and to that mother of hers. I interfered with both relationships. They were stronger or more important to Ginger than I was. It was fine while it lasted, except I often felt like an interloper. When it ended, I felt a bit sad and a lot relieved.

—Lew Ayres

I did not marry Jean-Paul Belmondo, though in every other way it was a marriage. I knew if we had taken vows and made a contract, it would have killed our passion. It would have ended the feeling of freedom that he needed....When we broke up, I wished I had a contract so he could pay me alimony for all the years I devoted to him! He got even more out of it than I did, believe me!

—Ursula Andress

☆ ☆ ☆ ☆

I should have married Rita Hayworth instead of Bette Davis. With Bette, it should have remained a love affair. When an affair burns itself out, it's best to make a clean break. But when the affair within a marriage—the sex—burns out, you're still stuck with each other, and things can turn very messy....My relationship with Rita might have lasted longer if we had been legally married. Unlike Bette, Rita was looking for a father figure, albeit a kindlier father figure than her own, who took advantage of her. Bette's father abandoned his family very early on, which is a kinder thing than to hang around and cause everyone grief and misery.

—Gary Merrill

☆ ☆ ☆ ☆

I loved Rita Hayworth. She was my lover, the mother of my daughter, and my wife, in that order. We never quite settled into a groove; we were too busy in those years. If we'd met sooner or if we'd met later in life, it might have worked out.

—Orson Welles

☆ ☆ ☆ ☆

My favorite husband? I've had several [five], but I really couldn't say, or I shouldn't say....I will confess it was nice being married to a crooner [Dick Haymes], when he sang to me....

—Rita Hayworth

☆ ☆ ☆ ☆

Two of my wives resented me because they thought I was better-looking than they were. That came out during one of our fights.

Another one resented that I looked younger than her. I can't help any of that. I thought I married pretty girls. Was I supposed to go marry someone like Mercedes McCambridge?

—Jeffrey Hunter

☆ ☆ ☆ ☆

My pal Carole Landis actually wanted to marry that scoundrel Rex Harrison. Probably you know the whole sordid story and how she finally killed herself over that lousy so-and-so. I never understood why so many gals are attracted to heels. I never met any guy who could convince me to give up my liberty or my life's pursuit of happiness!

—Patsy Kelly

☆ ☆ ☆ ☆

Four must be my unlucky number. I married [fourth husband] Ernest Borgnine in 1964, and about four weeks was all I could stand with the fella!

—Ethel Merman, whose marriage lasted less than a year

☆ ☆ ☆ ☆

Yes, we were married, but it only lasted a few months, so it's not really worth answering in detail.

—Troy Donahue on his 1964 marriage to Suzanne Pleshette

☆ ☆ ☆ ☆

Millions of people must think I'm married to Jim Backus, as I was on *Gilligan's Island.* (They played the Howells.) Jim is sweet, but I was married to one of Hollywood's most important character actors, Louis Calhern. He was very distinguished, and he was also one of Hollywood's most self-important actors.

—Natalie Schafer

☆ ☆ ☆ ☆

I begged Richard [Dawson] not to go to the States. You know what happens to most British actors who go there—they finish by playing butlers or opening fish-and-chips stands. With Dickie, it was worse: He became host of something called *Family Feud.*

—Diana Dors

☆ ☆ ☆ ☆

I lived with Jane Fonda, and I wanted to marry her. But she'd been very sheltered as a child, growing up inside Henry Fonda's mansion and in his giant, usually absent shadow. So Jane tended to come to things late—she married late, had a baby late, and woke up to politics late. She does what she does well, I do esteem her, but she's always been sort of a late bloomer....I still try to imagine how it might have been with us, together....

—James Franciscus

☆ ☆ ☆ ☆

I'm frequently asked what I saw in Mickey Rooney. In retrospect, I think one reason that I married him was what he saw in me....Don't forget, he was one of the biggest movie stars at the time, and I was fresh from the cotton and tobacco fields of North Carolina.

—Ava Gardner

☆ ☆ ☆ ☆

George C. Scott. Fine actor. Big drinker. Wife beater. What else do you want to know?

—Colleen Dewhurst

☆ ☆ ☆ ☆

I may not have gotten the girl in the movies, but in truth, I got Elizabeth Montgomery...and contrary to popular rumor, she is no witch. Just an enchantress.

—Gig Young

☆ ☆ ☆ ☆

My marriage to June Allyson means that whenever we have a tempest in a teapot—and we do!—it makes headlines, and they always exaggerate it, and I come off the heavy. June is America's sweetheart, so she always winds up smelling like a rose, no matter what.

—Dick Powell

☆ ☆ ☆ ☆

My marriage to Joan Fontaine roughly coincided with World War II. It even began the same year [1939]. Enough said?

—Brian Aherne

☆ ☆ ☆ ☆

I don't know the outcome of most mixed marriages, but it is difficult for most French-English couples. I did like and love Albert [Finney], but eventually our commitment was not as wide as what in English they call the English Channel....

—Anouk Aimée

☆ ☆ ☆ ☆

Eddie Albert is my handsome, charming *gringo*....I'm very proud to be Mexican, and Mexico has had one of the great cultures in world history, but I did not want a Mexican husband. A Mexican man, most of the time he just wants a servant or a mistress, and sometimes they are the same person—his wife! With an American man, there is the possibility of [being] equals. With a *Mexicano,* forget it!

—Margo

☆ ☆ ☆ ☆

[Mexican] Gilbert Roland was a wonderful husband. In one room of the house....

—Constance Bennett

☆ ☆ ☆ ☆

I am French, and in France we expect the wife to take a backseat. Or to sit somewhere besides the driver's seat. Even in the 1950s, before women's lib, Ginger Rogers was in our driver's seat. She wanted to play the conventional wife, but her stardom and her age (a sixteen-year age difference) would get in the way.

—Jacques Bergerac

I'm not married to a nationality, I'm married to a man.
>   —Candice Bergen on French director Louis Malle

☆ ☆ ☆ ☆

Jack's lucky to have me. He needs *someone* to keep him in line.
>   —Mary Livingstone on Jack Benny

☆ ☆ ☆ ☆

I was next-door neighbors with Jack Benny. The longer they were together, the shorter the leash she allowed him....Mary was a hard-hearted Hannah, while Jack was the dearest, drollest man.

>   —Lucille Ball

☆ ☆ ☆ ☆

The scuttlebutt was that Virginia Valli was more butch than Charles Farrell, ditto Mary Livingstone vis-à-vis Jack Benny. More than a few of your celebrated actor-actress marriages aren't entirely what they seem....

>   —David Niven

☆ ☆ ☆ ☆

Rudolph Valentino was no Italian stallion, at least where the ladies were concerned. He had two wives [both reportedly lesbian], but neither marriage took off. Apparently Rudy thought "consummate" meant to make soup.

>   —Rudy Vallee

☆ ☆ ☆ ☆

Janet Gaynor's husband was Adrian, the [M-G-M] fashion designer. But her wife was Mary Martin....

>   —Robert Cummings

☆ ☆ ☆ ☆

Joan Crawford thought we should get married. This was back in the 1920s, when I was a star and she was a rising flapper. It wasn't just a crass question of her ambition; we were very good but platonic friends. I told her, "Cranberry"—my pet name for her—"that isn't how it works in Hollywood. They usually pair men who like men and ladies who like ladies." Because if we *both* liked men, where would we be as man and wife? She'd resent me, and that would be the end of our beautiful friendship.

—William Haines

☆ ☆ ☆ ☆

I was closer to Clark Gable than any of his wives, except Carole Lombard, and we were a twosome longer than any of them. I would have married Clark if he'd asked me, but he thought we would overpower each other. He needed, frankly, a wife who wasn't as big a star as he was, though we did love each other dearly.

—Joan Crawford

☆ ☆ ☆ ☆

The unfortunate truth is, in this town men and women do compete....The happiest marriage I've seen in Hollywood is Billy Haines and Jimmy Shields.

—Joan Crawford

☆ ☆ ☆ ☆

I'm the only actor who ever married a congressman.
    —Melvyn Douglas on actress-turned-congresswoman Helen
Gahagan Douglas

☆ ☆ ☆ ☆

It started out well, but my marriage to Ida Lupino gradually became restrictive. This was even before she became famous as a lady director....I felt suffocated, like the title character in one of my most famous movies, *The Man in the Iron Mask.*

—Louis Hayward

☆ ☆ ☆ ☆

Rex [Harrison] is a very attentive husband. He's inclined to be somewhat too protective, but it's terribly flattering.

—Kay Kendall

Rex Harrison is so pompous, he expects a lady to open the door for *him*!

—Rachel Roberts

☆ ☆ ☆ ☆

You cannot believe how many letters the studio received over the years, urging that it pressure Greer Garson and myself into marriage! Some even urged that we divorce our respective spouses in order to be free to marry each other....That's when I learned that "fan" is short for "fanatic."

—Walter Pidgeon, Garson's frequent costar

☆ ☆ ☆ ☆

Janet Gaynor and I were always receiving wedding-anniversary presents in the mail, care of the studio. The fans didn't even know what date our anniversary fell on, which is logical, since we were never married!

—Charles Farrell, Gaynor's frequent costar

☆ ☆ ☆ ☆

I learned several tricks of the trade from my wife, Uta Hagen, one of the greatest acting teachers. But I never learned how to sing from Rosemary Clooney—we made children, not music, together.

—José Ferrer

☆ ☆ ☆ ☆

I'm on my sixth wife. I've married all kinds....What bugs me is when gossip tries to connect me with my [third] wife Lupe Velez [the Mexican Spitfire] and her tragic suicide. They have a crazy notion she killed herself over me. It had nothing at all to do with me. She killed herself over some French actor. It's a definite liability when you've been married to someone else who's famous and she died tragically. People concoct the craziest reasons!

—Johnny Weissmuller

☆ ☆ ☆ ☆

The men I married, I chose because they were intellectuals— Charlie Chaplin, Burgess Meredith, and Erich Maria Remarque.

They were my second, third, and fourth; I don't count my first husband—it wasn't memorable, and he was *not* an intellectual.

—Paulette Goddard

☆ ☆ ☆ ☆

Charlie [Bronson] isn't the handsomest man in the world, but he is very three-dimensional, and our marriage is for keeps.

—Jill Ireland

☆ ☆ ☆ ☆

In the first half of my life, I was best known as Florenz Ziegfeld's wife. In the second half, they remember me not as the great Ziegfeld's widow but as Glinda the Good [Witch in *The Wizard of Oz*].

—Billie Burke

☆ ☆ ☆ ☆

I never really thought I'd live so long that I wasn't known as Gracie Allen's husband.

—George Burns

☆ ☆ ☆ ☆

It didn't help our marriage when I became known as Barbra Streisand's husband. When we met, I was the leading man; she was the newcomer.

—Elliott Gould

☆ ☆ ☆ ☆

Betty Grable and Harry James! Folks think those two were born joined at the hip or born married. But before she was his wife, she was mine.

—Jackie Coogan (uncle Fester on TV's *Addams Family*)

☆ ☆ ☆ ☆

In Hollywood, you live in a fishbowl, and they make a big deal out of everything! I married Nicholas Ray, the director. People yawned, the press didn't care, although he was aces in his profession. Later on, I married his son, and from the press's reaction—and some of the public's, too—you'd have thought I was committing incest or robbing the cradle! *All* my marriages have been ordinary....

—Gloria Grahame

☆ ☆ ☆ ☆

People imagine I was the husband of Maria Montez, since we appeared in various pictures together. On her good days, Maria was fun to work with, but I couldn't have endured matrimony with her! I married another lovely Latin actress, Raquel Torres, who wasn't nearly as hypnotized by the silver screen as the immortal, tempestuous Maria.

—Jon Hall

☆ ☆ ☆ ☆

Richard Gere and Cindy Crawford. Such a pair, and what a concept—his body's by Nautilus and her mind's by Mattel.

—Sam Kinison

☆ ☆ ☆ ☆

Why do rock stars like Bruce Springsteen and Rod Stewart always wed blondes and models? Why don't they ever marry someone like Janis Joplin or Bette Midler? You want to know why? Those guys know they aren't *that* talented. They couldn't stand the comparisons.

—Jill Ireland

☆ ☆ ☆ ☆

Some of his female fans criticized Robert Taylor for marrying Barbara Stanwyck. Some of them felt she was too old for him; a few years' age discrepancy back then was much commented upon. Others thought he was too pretty for her. But I tell you this: They were flat-out relieved that he married *someone*....

—William Haines

☆ ☆ ☆ ☆

I married a designer [Oleg Cassini]. The thing is, I wasn't the only person he had designs on.

—Gene Tierney

Did John F. Kennedy propose to me? I think you're aware of the answer [yes]....The fact is, had he married me, he couldn't have had the political career that he did. In those days, it was that simple.

—Gene Tierney

☆ ☆ ☆ ☆

When I became known to American filmgoers [for *The Seventh Veil* with James Mason], some of the columnists there hinted that I would do very well for myself and my career if I married James Mason. This, without even checking my marital status! I would never have married for such a philistine reason....One of my husbands was [director] David Lean. I acted in a number of his films, but that was a by-product of the marriage, not the reason for it.

—Ann Todd

☆ ☆ ☆ ☆

I moved from Czechoslovakia to German films to Broadway to Hollywood. My wife, Margo, had trouble pronouncing the letter "v," and she once remarked on a radio interview, "My husband is a slob." She was really saying, "My husband is a Slav." Thereafter, I asked her to refrain from describing my background in public. Also to avoid mention in public of Shakespeare's play *Richard III*. She had pronounced it, luckily at home, as "Richard the Turd."

—Francis Lederer

☆ ☆ ☆ ☆

Elvis Presley confided in me soon after he did *Viva Las Vegas* with Ann-Margret that he was considering marrying her. I'm not implying that anything untoward ever occurred between them, but they had a marvelous chemistry. But soon after that, I think he might have had it read to him from a review, he heard Ann-Margret described as "a female Elvis," and Elvis reacted negatively. To his mind, it was vaguely homosexual! Whether that's what cooled his feelings for Ann-Margret or not, I don't know.

—Bobby Darin

☆ ☆ ☆ ☆

I do feel a little sorry for Gene Raymond. He is one of the few child actors who did make it into adult stardom. In the 1930s he was a matinee idol, handsome, blond....He married Jeanette [MacDonald], and theirs has been a rare and successful Hollywood marriage, but these days most of the public who are under thirty know Gene more for his marriage than his own outstanding career.

—Nelson Eddy

☆ ☆ ☆ ☆

Al Jolson was my first husband. He used to boast that he was spoiling me for any man who might come after him. I think Al sensed that it wasn't easy for me being married to an American institution....Was he right about spoiling me? I'm sorry, I couldn't possibly say. I couldn't be that indiscreet.

—Ruby Keeler

☆ ☆ ☆ ☆

I did experience some resentment from fans at premieres that we attended when I was married to Dick Powell. I got to hear them blurt out, "Where's Ruby?" They either thought he should be married to [his frequent costar] Ruby Keeler, or they may have thought he was, and goodness knows what they thought *I* was to him!

—Joan Blondell

☆ ☆ ☆ ☆

I *was* married to Glenn Ford. But now I feel as though I'm married to God, and in the nicest, purest sense.

—dancer-actress Eleanor Powell, who became an ordained minister

☆ ☆ ☆ ☆

My fourth husband was an actor [Gary Merrill]. We had tremendous fights. He used his fists more than his mouth....It was a hell of a marriage, even the making up. They ought to rewrite the ceremony—"in sickness and in hell..."

—Bette Davis

Life with Maria [Montez] was like living on the edge of a volcano. Except that, of course, she was much better-looking than the average volcano.

—Jean-Pierre Aumont

Bette Davis makes up

I was just really young. I don't know what his excuse is, but that's mine.

—Winona Ryder on her breakup with Johnny Depp

☆ ☆ ☆ ☆

I hear Jane Fonda is friends with her first husband [director Roger Vadim], because she left him. But that she is not friends with her second husband [politician Tom Hayden], because he left her. So we will have to wait and see who leaves who with her new husband Ted Turner. It's all a matter of time....

—Ursula Andress

☆ ☆ ☆ ☆

He's a wuss....He sucks. Yes....Well, yes.

—Butthead (of Beavis & Butthead) and Cher on her ex-husband Sonny Bono

☆ ☆ ☆ ☆

She was twelve years old. She had sex with another girl in the neighborhood. I don't know if I would call that a lesbian affair....Roseanne has not been having lesbian affairs during our marriage.

—Tom Arnold

☆ ☆ ☆ ☆

Lavender Limelight

Why don't you put that in the headline: "He Only Did Three [movies] With Doris [Day]!" Set a lot of people straight.
—Rock Hudson

☆ ☆ ☆ ☆

If Liberace is straight, then I'm a Dutchman!
—Paul Lynde

☆ ☆ ☆ ☆

Liberace and Truman Capote—I can never get those two straight.
—Milton Berle

☆ ☆ ☆ ☆

I saw Wayne Newton and Liberace together in a pink bathtub. What do you think that meant?
—Johnny Carson

☆ ☆ ☆ ☆

Truman Capote is a Republican housewife from Kansas with all the prejudices.
—Gore Vidal

143

Gore Vidal has never written a novel that's readable, with the exception of *Myra Breckenridge,* which you can sort of thumb your way through....His novels are unbelievably bad. His essays are quite good...if he doesn't *hate* somebody too much.

—Truman Capote

☆ ☆ ☆ ☆

Kay Francis was shown falling in love with an officer [in *Four Jills in a Jeep*]. This was a tribute to her acting skill, because she had very little interest in men.

—Phil Silvers

☆ ☆ ☆ ☆

Garbo and I starred in *Grand Hotel,* but we had no scenes together. Alas. For her, and her alone, I could have been a lesbian.

—Joan Crawford

☆ ☆ ☆ ☆

Greta Garbo felt comfortable at *my* parties....Beatrice Lillie also came. She was called the funniest woman in the world, and she was the one person who could make Garbo laugh at will. Garbo thought her adorable and endlessly amusing and envied her her short, boyish haircut.

—George Cukor

☆ ☆ ☆ ☆

Bea's passion [in Hollywood] was directed at Greta Garbo, the first woman she'd ever seen who wore slacks in public.

—Sheilah Graham

☆ ☆ ☆ ☆

I wouldn't mind having had an affair with Marlene Dietrich when she was young. Like, who wouldn't?

—Madonna

☆ ☆ ☆ ☆

They called him "Ravishing Ramón," and he was so popular and handsome that long before he turned twenty-five, the reporters

would ask him why he never married. He always told them he had considered becoming a priest. He said he was still thinking about becoming a father. Only thing is, he was fooling around with the wrong gender if he really wanted to become a father!
—Fernando Lamas on Ramón Novarro

☆ ☆ ☆ ☆

He certainly is a gay caballero. That means "gentleman." He's gay and a caballero, all right.
—Lee Marvin on Cantinflas

☆ ☆ ☆ ☆

Sandy [Dennis] feared being physically penetrated. Her closest relationships were with cats and gay men.
—director James Bridges

☆ ☆ ☆ ☆

[Raymond Burr] uses the same trick a lot of Latin American actors, singers, and writers use—he invents wives and offspring for himself so people will believe him heterosexual.
—Emlyn (*The Corn Is Green*) Williams

☆ ☆ ☆ ☆

It's ironic that Hedda Hopper was such a homophobe. She tried to yank Cary Grant out of the closet and printed that Michael Wilding [Elizabeth Taylor's second husband] and Stewart Granger had had an affair. Yet her only child [actor William Hopper of *Perry Mason*] was in love with Raymond Burr. You know who told me so? Lucille Ball. Lucy wasn't right wing, but she and Hedda Hopper were very good friends, and Hedda told Lucy all the latest gossip—except about Bill Hopper.
—gossip columnist Joyce Haber

☆ ☆ ☆ ☆

...That dyke!
—Elizabeth Taylor in Marilyn Monroe's presence, as reported by Norman Mailer

☆ ☆ ☆ ☆

Closet legal case: Raymond Burr

Madonna and Sandra Bernhard? That's like Paul Newman and Woody Allen. Or Jerri Hall and Mick Jagger.

—Boy George

☆ ☆ ☆ ☆

In the sixties, we all had crushes on Nureyev, but I went further. I proposed cohabitation. He said no; I was too old for him.

—Cecil Beaton

☆ ☆ ☆ ☆

Alfred Lunt is an actor who has his head in the clouds and his feet in the box office.

—Noel Coward

☆ ☆ ☆ ☆

Everyone in New York City knows that Tony Perkins's marriage is just a front. He still has male lovers.... Tony couldn't settle down with another guy because he's insecure and craves kinky affairs, not a genuine or lasting relationship. Tony isn't exactly Norman Bates [of *Psycho*], but he's awfully kinky....

—Halston

☆ ☆ ☆ ☆

I'd always heard around town that Robert Taylor was bisexual, that his marriage to Barbara Stanwyck was arranged, and that she was also gay. So when I met Taylor, I figured we'd have something in common, right? Wrong! I was open, he was not only closeted, he was right wing and a witch-hunter, not at all friendly or honest or even smiling.

—Sal Mineo

☆ ☆ ☆ ☆

My favorite American lesbian!

—Clifton Webb on Barbara Stanwyck

☆ ☆ ☆ ☆

Let me tell you something that Mae West said. She was asked about the men she was seen with in public. And she replied, "It's not the men you see me with, it's the men you don't see me with...." That is true of everybody in public life, especially the sexually uncommon....

—Cecil Beaton

☆ ☆ ☆ ☆

I always heard that Noel Coward wrote that song ["Mad About the Boy"] because of his friend Cary Grant....

—Douglas Fairbanks Jr.

☆ ☆ ☆ ☆

I always heard from the girls that he [Fred Astaire] was not such a hot dance partner at parties. He was very shy, and he much preferred the company of men.

—Douglas Fairbanks Jr.

☆ ☆ ☆ ☆

[Filming *The Man Who Would Be King*]: We were in this little town on the edge of the Sahara, and there was nothing to do at night except go to this disco. But it was all men dancing with men because women weren't allowed out at night. So we're standing at the bar, watching all these guys dancing, when Sean [Connery] leans over and says to me, "Do you mind if I dance with your driver? Mine's too ugly."

—Michael Caine

☆ ☆ ☆ ☆

I knew her better than a husband would....

—Beatrice Lillie on Gertrude Lawrence

☆ ☆ ☆ ☆

Noel [Coward] and I were in Paris once. Adjoining rooms, of course. One night, I felt mischievous, so I knocked on Noel's door, and he asked, "Who is it?" I lowered my voice and said, "Hotel detective. Have you got a gentleman in your room?" He answered, "Just a minute, I'll ask him."

—Beatrice Lillie

Bea Lillie is so enchantingly fey, she can do anything. I should love to perform [Lillie's signature song] "There Are Fairies at the Bottom of Our Garden," but I don't dare. It might come out "There Are Fairies in the Garden of My Bottom."

—Noel Coward

☆ ☆ ☆ ☆

I did consider marrying Tyrone Power. But I decided he was too fond of the boys for it to work out.

—Alice Faye

☆ ☆ ☆ ☆

I heard Gene Kelly in an interview, a very interesting interview, and I thought it was a dead giveaway. He said, "You know, it's a shame that a guy can't dance without being called a homosexual," and then went into this long routine defending himself—you know, "I'm married and have kids...."

—Louise Brooks

☆ ☆ ☆ ☆

When we did *Rebel Without a Cause,* Nick Adams told me he and James Dean had a big affair—I don't know if it was while they were living together or not. There's always the roomie thing in Hollywood—Brando and Wally Cox, Brando and Tony Curtis, Cary Grant and Randolph Scott—and there are always rumors about them, even if they aren't true....I think Hollywood secretly *wants* to think it's true. Such handsome couples....

—Sal Mineo

☆ ☆ ☆ ☆

Brando. Always, one wants Brando—for everything, one wants him....

—director Luchino Visconti

☆ ☆ ☆ ☆

Brando told me that Jimmy Dean used to call him on the phone all the time, and Marlon would listen to him talking to the

Marlon Brando leans on his fan, James Dean

answering service, and he wouldn't answer, wouldn't speak up.
This was one of the more disgusting aspects of Marlon's. Marlon
was just getting frightened....

—Truman Capote

☆ ☆ ☆ ☆

Ray [Bolger] does it all. He acts, dances, sings, is a great
comedian, and he's president of the Ray Bolger Fan Club. About
the only thin' he doesn't do is ball chicks. He says dancin' and
exercise take care of all those needs, but I heard some pretty
perversive [sic] rumors about that guy's love life!

—Desi Arnaz

☆ ☆ ☆ ☆

An old queen from way, way back. [Comedian] Billy [De Wolfe]
was great—he could break up anyone....As the *New York Times*
would say, "A confirmed bachelor."

—Rock Hudson

No one remembers that she [Isadora Duncan] flirted with everyone, both sexes alike. I was a mere slip of a girl at the time, yet she made a pass at me. I was sophisticated enough to recognize it for what it was but young enough to decline!...Later, I heard rumors about some of her lady friends in Gay Paree....

—Elsa Lanchester

☆ ☆ ☆ ☆

Monsieur Chevalier and I did a mature love duet in *Gigi*. Quite mature—a song of senility, really....He was not without talent, I can tell you, for he enacted an old boy who'd once been in love with me and a few hundred other females. And off the screen, Maurice was not really enamored of any performer with a bosom.

—Hermione Gingold

☆ ☆ ☆ ☆

I got a message from Aretha Franklin saying she'd love to do a song with me. Later, after she'd done the [duet] with George Michael, the London *Evening Standard* asked me if I thought she'd called the wrong George. I said, "I think she banged on the wrong closet."

—Boy George

☆ ☆ ☆ ☆

That girl Pat Hernandez whom he's with was my fag hag for three years, and when I read the newspaper story "How Pat Broke My Heart," I was tempted to write one called "How Pat Broke My Hoover" [vacuum cleaner]. Because the idea of her and George Michael having a relationship is about as likely as my having sex with a door.

—Boy George

☆ ☆ ☆ ☆

I was at a urinal once, next to Milton Berle, who is renowned in Hollywood, and I don't mean just for his comedy! I'm a big man on campus myself. I looked down at Milton, then looked back at the wall, and to relieve the tension, I said, "If Truman Capote were here, he'd be singing "Stranger in Paradise."

—Sammy Davis Jr.

I took drugs, not a lot, back when I was friends with Aldous
Huxley. Mostly, I took drugs to please Cary Grant. He was trying
LSD, back when it was legal. He had the notion that he could
become heterosexual with it. I didn't do anything heavy-duty,
just some trivial drugs, because Cary didn't want to do his thing
solo—he was a very lonely man. Very insecure—obviously. I'm
so secure, it's ridiculous!

—Truman Capote

☆ ☆ ☆ ☆

Anthony Perkins is awful, I can't stand him. There's nothing
there, and he pretends not to know if he's really gay or not. Just
ask any one of the small army of his ex-lovers! Of which *I* am not
one! I don't like blood, and Tony's a sadist. He likes to see blood. I
mean, he *is* Norman Bates!

—Truman Capote

☆ ☆ ☆ ☆

I did work for [George Bernard] Shaw. Which rather dates
me....Mr. Shaw was born old. I was not....He was rumored to
be neutral about sex. I certainly couldn't say whether he was
celibate or only said it to shock. I'd like to know what Freud
might have thought of him....Shaw would have made a perfect
priest, except he happened to be an atheist.

—Estelle Winwood

☆ ☆ ☆ ☆

We lived in fear of an exposé, or even one small remark, a veiled
suggestion that someone was homosexual. Such a remark would
have caused an earthquake at the studio....The amazing thing is
that Rock [Hudson], as big as he became, was never nailed. It
made one speculate that Rock had an angel on his shoul-
der....He seemed under supernatural protection.

—George Nader

☆ ☆ ☆ ☆

Rock Hudson was emotionally constipated. He hated having to
play hetero on screen, he hated having to pretend offscreen, and
he hated anyone saying he was gay. We acted together, but we

could never have socialized. I let it all hang out; he left it all hanging in. And now that he's not a big star anymore, he's still just as uptight!

—Paul Lynde

☆ ☆ ☆ ☆

Of course I knew Laurence Olivier and Danny Kaye were having a long-term affair. So did all of London. So did their wives. Why is America always the last to know?

—Peggy Ashcroft

☆ ☆ ☆ ☆

Listen, the love between two men is beautiful. I'd love to be between, say, Tyrone Power and Montgomery Clift.... Hell, I was born the wrong gender!

—Nancy Walker

☆ ☆ ☆ ☆

In the two books about Monty they have things about [actor] Kevin McCarthy and what a great friend he was to Monty. And in the books, McCarthy says he had no *idea* that Monty Clift was homosexual and was absolutely *amazed*....Why, he said, it never crossed his mind. Well, it had crossed the mind of every single trolley-car conductor in Hollywood, so it was very difficult to believe it hadn't crossed the mind of his best friend for seven and a half years. I mean, how far can hypocrisy go?

—Truman Capote

☆ ☆ ☆ ☆

Lily Tomlin has been in and out of the closet more times than my hunting jacket.

—Rock Hudson

☆ ☆ ☆ ☆

I heard that my *Darling Lili* taskmasters, Blake Edwards and Julie Andrews, were implying to the press that I'm gay. I could hardly believe it! Talk about the kettle calling the pot black!

—Rock Hudson

Mary Martin was Broadway's biggest closet king. Everyone thought Ethel [Merman] was butch and maybe a lesbian, but she wasn't. And everyone thought that lovely little Mary was Miss Femme, and she was—except next to her gay husband [Richard Halliday]. In other words, don't judge a star by her cover.

—Bob Fosse

☆ ☆ ☆ ☆

The whole world knows Agnes [Moorehead] was a lesbian—I mean, classy as hell, but one of the all-time Hollywood dykes.

—Paul Lynde

☆ ☆ ☆ ☆

The only thing that dikey bitch and I ever had in common was Billie Burke [aka Glinda the Good Witch], who supported both of us in our first pictures.

—Margaret Sullavan on Katharine Hepburn

☆ ☆ ☆ ☆

Barbara Stanwyck loved doing westerns more than anything where she had to dress up frilly and chase after a man. At heart, she's a cowgirl. Or a cowboy—she's one of the toughest, most no-nonsense women in this town, and she stopped playing the old cat-and-mouse game years ago.

—Walter Huston

☆ ☆ ☆ ☆

I was a guest once at Eleanor Roosevelt's place. I saw this pink nightgown and just for a gag put it on over my clothes. Noel Coward walks in and says, "My dear, you look simply di-vine!," and kisses my hand. Next time I see Eleanor at a party she says loudly, "Why, Bob, last time we met you were in a pink nightgown being kissed by Noel Coward!" What could I do but admit it?

—Robert Mitchum

☆ ☆ ☆ ☆

I lived with Don Johnson, I discovered him, put him in a play set in prison with a gay theme (*Fortune and Men's Eyes*). I lived with both Don and his sister, and people imagined all sorts of things.... I'll put it like this: Yes, I'm bisexual, and blond guys are my favorite type, and I did enjoy seeing Don nude on the stage, and on the silver screen, for that matter. Who wouldn't? So what?

—Sal Mineo

☆ ☆ ☆ ☆

That German actress [Marlene Dietrich] wanted to wash my hair. She came into my dressing room—we were both at Paramount—and made the offer. I had to turn her down—I was afraid she didn't mean the hair on my head....

—Mae West

☆ ☆ ☆ ☆

Cheetah bit me whenever he could. The [Tarzan] apes were all homosexuals, eager to wrap their paws around Johnny Weismuller's thighs. They were jealous of me, and I loathed them.

—Maureen ("Jane") O'Sullivan

☆ ☆ ☆ ☆

They're so handsome, I could be bisexual for them.
—Burt Reynolds (to Barbara Walters) re Ryan O'Neal and other actors and male models, including the Marlboro Man (played by Tom Selleck)

☆ ☆ ☆ ☆

I got fed up with Twentieth Century-Fox and Hollywood when Marilyn Monroe came on the scene and they actually built her up into this giant of tiny proportions. The things they let her get away with! On account of the money she made for them. For instance, she took direction not from her directors but her lesbian drama coach, whom they all said she was sleeping with. That's none of my concern, but it got my goat when they took a no-talent and began ignoring those of us who could actually act!

—Anne Baxter

☆ ☆ ☆ ☆

I think Eve Arden was great in two things: *Stage Door* (costarring Lucille Ball) and *Our Miss Brooks* (produced by Desilu). The rest of her career, you could have. Not me. I never wanted to play a man. I'm not going to repeat any rumors I've heard, but on the screen she almost never played a woman. Sure, she was funny at times, if you went for that kind of humor....

—Lucille Ball

☆ ☆ ☆ ☆

Did you know Dolores Del Rio's first two husbands were queer? The first was a Mexican. He shot himself. The second was M-G-M's self-inflated art director Cedric Gibbons. I never did get around to asking her why she never had children. Or whether she wanted any.

—David Niven

☆ ☆ ☆ ☆

Dennis Hopper says James Dean was not gay. Maybe he's right insofar as Jimmy was bisexual. But he definitely was not heterosexual, and he preferred men who could dominate him, which is why he worshipped Marlon Brando—besides Brando's huge talent. You have to remember, a lot of guys in Hollywood that swung both ways in their youth grow into conservative and scared older men, and they not only deny stuff about themselves but about anyone they knew well.

—Peter Allen

☆ ☆ ☆ ☆

I was one of Monty's [Clift] best friends. I know that James Dean admired Monty's talent and looks, but he didn't have much more than a passing crush on him, let alone a grand passion for him. Monty and Jimmy were far too much alike in their sexual desires to be attractive to each other. And too masochistic.

—Nancy Walker

☆ ☆ ☆ ☆

Ernest Hemingway was basically a homosexual putting on a fighting-and-fucking act to fool himself.

—Louise Brooks

All About Eve?—Arden and Audrey Long in "Pan Americana"

Cedric Gibbons, Dolores Del Rio, and David Niven

Hemingway and I were never lovers. It was too special for that....

—Marlene Dietrich

☆ ☆ ☆ ☆

Richard Simmons is carrying Rex Reed's baby.

—Andy Warhol

☆ ☆ ☆ ☆

Richard Simmons is to exercise what Liberace is to piano playing.

—Gilda Radner

☆ ☆ ☆ ☆

His name is Prince, but he dresses like a princess.

—Halston

I knew right away that Rock Hudson was gay when he did not fall in love with me.

—Gina Lollobrigida

☆ ☆ ☆ ☆

David Bowie is an opportunist. He came out of the closet before any other music star, but he's also the only one I've ever heard of that went back in....

—Peter Allen

☆ ☆ ☆ ☆

Rock Hudson surrounded himself with fellow closet queens, horrible, selfish, self-loathing older men. The day after Rock died of AIDS, one of them went on national TV to say Rock had died of anorexia, and another went on TV to deny that Rock was gay! This was all by way of saving their own silly skins, staying in that closet forever....

—Peter Allen

☆ ☆ ☆ ☆

I'll always remember going out for dinner with him [David Bowie] and Angie....It was a fabulous evening, and over dinner he admitted to me that he always wanted to be Judy Garland, and that's the God's honest truth.

—Elton John

☆ ☆ ☆ ☆

I thought about what I contributed toward variety—and the only important thing is I danced with Elton John.

—Sir John Gielgud, on receiving a Variety Club Award

☆ ☆ ☆ ☆

One thing Cary Grant did admit when we worked together—the two of us, sitting talking between scenes—was that he had a crush on Elvis Presley. He didn't say the word "crush," but that's clearly what he meant. I'd heard tales that Howard Hughes had been more than Grant's best man, that they were very close, but I didn't pursue that.... Our movie together was the last one Cary Grant acted in, but a few years later he did one more movie, in which he appeared as himself, which in some ways was his hardest role. It was an Elvis documentary (*Elvis—That's the Way It Is*).

—Jim Hutton

☆ ☆ ☆ ☆

It is not wonderful for everybody to come out of their closets. Not everybody is a good asset to gays. Franco Zeffirelli is out of the closet, I read, but maybe he should stay back in....

—Rudolf Nureyev

☆ ☆ ☆ ☆

Gays are people first. Most aren't extraordinary. Some are heroes, many are sexy, and some are nothing but villains, like J. Edgar Hoover and Roy Cohn. We can't all be Alexander the Great or look like Tyrone Power.

—Tennessee Williams

☆ ☆ ☆ ☆

Danny Kaye—it rhymes with "gay."...

—Paul Lynde

☆ ☆ ☆ ☆

Now I hear Laurence Olivier had a big affair with Danny Kaye. I can't believe it! I know opposites are alleged to attract, but what did Sir Laurence see in Danny Kaye, of all people? His wacky sense of humor? I can't even picture it.

—Sandy Dennis

☆ ☆ ☆ ☆

If I'm reincarnated, I want to come back as Matt Dillon's underwear.

—Boy George

☆ ☆ ☆ ☆

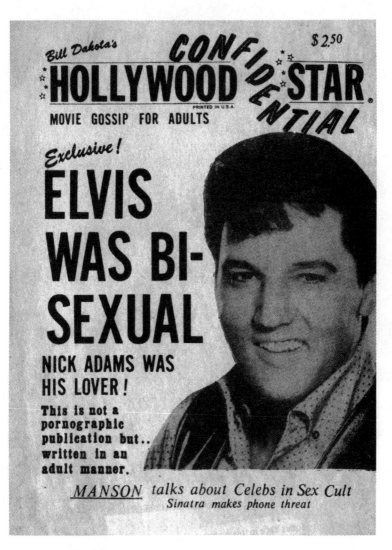

Elvis: Autosexual!

(Boy George, mad about) Matt Dillon

Conrad Veidt....Sober, he was straight. Drunk, he was homosexual.

—Robert Helpmann

☆ ☆ ☆ ☆

Larry [Olivier] was jealous of my friendship with Vivien [Leigh]. He was intimidated by me and afraid of me. He was afraid to become friends with me due to what that might suggest to others whose opinions he valued *so* highly.

—Robert Helpmann

I love men! I had four husbands, for Christ's sake!
—Bette Davis's reply when Elizabeth Taylor asked if there
were any truth to the rumor of an affair with Mary Astor

☆ ☆ ☆ ☆

I love golf, though I'm not wild about all of the females who play
it. Just because I'm out on the links, don't get the wrong
impression. For me, it's a pasttime, not a way of life. Don't
confuse me with Vilma Banky.

—Mary Astor

☆ ☆ ☆ ☆

Dinah Shore's a heterosexual, but her golf tournament is probably the biggest sapphic event of the year, in sports. It brings in
twenty thousand to forty thousand lesbians to Palm Springs.
Suddenly, the place becomes *where the girls are....*

—Martina Navratilova

☆ ☆ ☆ ☆

Rock Hudson let his gay agent marry him off to his secretary
because he didn't want people to get the right idea.

—Anthony Perkins

☆ ☆ ☆ ☆

Sometimes you can tell which actors are gay because they're so
terrified of being disclosed or discloseted that they keep on
marrying, right up to their death. Especially when it's an old
dude like Cary Grant or Fred Astaire and the wife is decades
younger. It's not a marriage of winter passion; it's a marriage of
eternal image....Cary Grant I know for a fact was gay. Astaire, I
don't know; I question whether he was anything. But it was
desperately, pathetically, important to both men that they continue to be thought of as heterosexual.

—Halston

☆ ☆ ☆ ☆

I'm not saying every Richard Chamberlain or Cesar Romero is
gay. There do happen to be some lifelong heterosexual bach-

elors. But, generally speaking, and particularly in Hollywood, where the pressure to wed and to pass is intense, if an actor is over fifty, or eighty, and he hasn't married, the chances are that he's part of the brotherhood.

—director Colin Higgins

☆ ☆ ☆ ☆

Johnny Mathis came out of the closet. Why does that seem redundant?

—Johnnie Ray

☆ ☆ ☆ ☆

What a liar! Honey, even a blind man could see Liberace was gay.

—Peter Allen

☆ ☆ ☆ ☆

Louis B. Mayer ordered Nelson Eddy to marry. Eddy agreed, but he didn't want a virgin bride or some insatiable creature, and Mayer understood. Sometimes the least sexual marriages last the longest, so long as it's mutual....Mayer found him an older divorcée who'd been married to a movie director—she was wise to the ways of Tinseltown, she was not sexually demanding or needful, and she was well pleased to live the comfortable life of a movie star's wife. She was satisfied, Eddy was satisfied, the studio was satisfied, the public was satisfied. At least I *assume* Nelson Eddy was satisfied. For his sake, I hope he had a very low sex drive. Or perhaps he was very, very discreet if he did step out....

—Noel Coward

☆ ☆ ☆ ☆

One of the more closeted famous designers here in New York told me that he used to see Nelson Eddy at the Turkish baths ogling the young men. He felt free to ogle in New York but never in Los Angeles. This designer said he once flirted with Eddy, but the poor guy became too nervous and left. Either he never did anything but look, or he had to be the one to do the flirting....Nelson Eddy's rather ironic nickname at that baths was "Naughty Marietta" (after a 1935 Eddy-MacDonald movie), but there was little or no evidence that poor Nelson ever got up the nerve to act "naughty"!

—Halston

☆ ☆ ☆ ☆

Nelson Eddy and I worked together in *The Phantom of the Opera*. I didn't get to know him on a personal level. But he wasn't as dull as some of his critics had suggested. To give you an illustration, he didn't even flirt with his leading lady or the supporting female players. Now, in pictures, every gentleman star makes eyes at his leading lady, if only to be polite. It's practically in the contract! So Mr. Eddy's behavior was very interesting indeed....

—Claude Rains

☆ ☆ ☆ ☆

Elsa Maxwell, the hostess with the mostest, was probably Hollywood's most renowned lesbian. Of course, she wasn't in the movies; she couldn't have been, the way she looked...or as relatively open as she was about her private life....If Elsa had been a beauty, she'd have had a chance of getting in the movies, and in that case, I'm sure she'd have feigned to have a boyfriend. She could be freer than the actresses because she wasn't obligated to a movie contract with its "morals clause," and because she wasn't a figure men dreamed and fantasized about.

—Merle Oberon

☆ ☆ ☆ ☆

When he was asked why he never married, Ramón Novarro always trotted out that stock answer—he'd long considered becoming a priest. The intention was to make readers think he was still celibate. Far from it!

—George Cukor

☆ ☆ ☆ ☆

Clifton Webb was fascinating to watch and listen to, a born wit. He was his own greatest creation...his roles were all molded in his own personality....He never married, but nobody would think of bringing up *that* topic. However, I heard that a director once asked him, face-to-face, "Are you a homosexual?" and Webb replied, "Devout!"

—Stephen Boyd

☆ ☆ ☆ ☆

I've heard or read about actors being asked the immortal question "Why have you never married?" They answer with the immortal excuse "I just haven't found the right girl." Because I'm on the hefty side [up to three hundred pounds], no one's asked me yet. If they do, that's the answer I'll give. After all, if it's good enough for Monty Clift and Sal Mineo....

—Victor Buono

☆ ☆ ☆ ☆

Oh, dear. I've got to go through another day of kissing John Gilbert.

—Lillian Gish, arriving on the set of *La Bohème* (1926)

☆ ☆ ☆ ☆

She is the most repetitive interview subject! She's always bemoaning the death of silent movies...feels that talkies are vastly inferior to silents!...And on the subject of why she never got married, she always says it's because she didn't want to "ruin" some "dear man's" life. Brother!

—Bette Davis on Lillian Gish

☆ ☆ ☆ ☆

I don't know if this pertains to Marlene Dietrich or to Eleanor Roosevelt, but one of them reportedly said it. When she found out that her husband was cheating on her, the wife said, "Well, if he has a mistress, I'm going to have one, too!"

—Fernando Lamas

☆ ☆ ☆ ☆

Marlene Dietrichs [sic]....She is like a female Greta Garbo. And she sings, too!

—Paramount mogul Adolph Zukor

She was ugly, fat, and a lesbian, but she collected more loot than all the jewels of Liz Taylor, Marlene, and mine rolled together.
—Paulette Goddard on Gertrude Stein's valuable art collection

☆ ☆ ☆ ☆

Hey, I'm never surprised when an Englishman or some hunk actor is discovered to be homosexual. Where's the surprise in that? But I'll tell you what nearly knocked me out of my chair—when I found out Grandpa Walton [Will Geer] was gay! Grandpa Walton...he even looked like Uncle Sam.

—Forrest Tucker

☆ ☆ ☆ ☆

How Hollywood has changed! The lesbian and homosexual stars lived in abject terror of Louella Parsons and Hedda Hopper hinting that they were queer....Miss Hopper got bolder and bolder about what today is called "outing." She tried to do it to Cary Grant, but he was too big a star to be jeopardized, even by her. She did allege, later, that there had been an affair between Stewart Granger and Elizabeth Taylor's intended, Michael Wilding....Today's queer stars—sorry, *gay* stars—can rest much easier. The gossip columnists who count are three thousand miles away, in New York (Liz Smith, Cindy Adams], or they're openly gay themselves—I refer to the three Hollywood Kids. Sorry, *two*—one of them was stricken [by AIDS], wasn't he?

—Terry-Thomas

☆ ☆ ☆ ☆

Quite by accident, I once picked up a copy of an American gossip magazine called *The Advocate*. I thought it curious that a legal journal should feature gossip and mostly drivel; then I saw by the tawdry personals [ads] that it was a gay rag! I *had* to read it then, out of morbid interest. My jaw dropped to the floor when I read a purported interview with Robert Morse in which he allegedly admitted to bisexuality! I had appeared with Mr. Morse in a dismal Doris Day picture called *Where Were You When the Lights Went Out?* Where was my *mind* when I accepted that role? I didn't know whether to believe it. But then I went on to learn that Mr. Morse is the father of five...so I'm rather in the fog. I do know one thing: I would *not* have believed it if they'd said he was homosexual and a father of five! That would stretch my credulity to the breaking point!

—Terry-Thomas

☆ ☆ ☆ ☆

I worked more than once with the great Dame Margaret Rutherford. She always managed to get her husband [Stringer Davis] a small role in her latest picture. I'm not telling tales out of school, for everyone knows it was a marriage of convenience. They each derived an emotional benefit out of their nonphysical union. Rather like that famous quote of Katharine Hepburn's about Fred Astaire—she said that in her films he gave Ginger Rogers class and she gave him sex. Not literally, of course!

—Terry-Thomas

☆ ☆ ☆ ☆

Kenneth Williams is the stereotype of the comedian who's laughing on the outside and crying on the inside. All he'd have to do to be happy is to get laid. But he can't bring himself to do that. He'd rather be celibate than be disapproved of.

—playwright Joe Orton

☆ ☆ ☆ ☆

It was an open secret that Richard Deacon was homosexual. He neither confirmed nor denied....Oddly enough, if his persona had been more fun and flamboyant, like Charles Nelson Reilly or Paul Lynde, he'd probably have gotten more work after the series went off the air. Richard was awfully taciturn, very wry. He was a much better straight man—so to speak—than a comic actor. Few of the public guessed his secret.
One of the people on our series was not so subtly homophobic and used to make little jabs at Richard, which he shrugged off, although I'm certain he felt them deeply...and another person on our series was, and is, homosexual, but you'll never get that individual's name out of me!

—*Dick Van Dyke Show* director and costar Jerry Paris

When they offered me a part on *The Dick Van Dyke Show* (D.V.D. was a relative newcomer], I asked, "What's a Dick Van Dyke?"
—Rose-Marie

☆ ☆ ☆ ☆

I was a professional sissy, but when I joined the Three Stooges, I became world-famous. But it bothered me what people thought....Because the best professional sissies are perfectly normal men! They didn't have to place me in the same category as Liberace. Liberace wasn't an actor....
—Joe Besser

☆ ☆ ☆ ☆

Johnny Carson has a heterosexual second banana [Ed McMahon], and Merv Griffin had a homosexual one [Arthur Treacher].
—George Rose

☆ ☆ ☆ ☆

TV in America doesn't exactly keep up with the times. It's a bigot's medium. The only *out* gay performer on American TV is Scott Thompson (of *Kids in the Hall*), and almost nobody's heard of him, so he has nothing to lose by being honest.
—Peter Allen

☆ ☆ ☆ ☆

Nobody is that fem.
—Disney juvenile star Tommy Kirk on Little Richard

☆ ☆ ☆ ☆

Elvis may have been the king of rock 'n roll, but I am the queen!
—Little Richard

☆ ☆ ☆ ☆

Michael Jackson!
—Little Richard's one and only choice to play him in a movie of his life

I may look like a darker, shorter Liberace, but honey, we are *not* soul sisters.

—the uncloseted Sylvester

☆ ☆ ☆ ☆

[In the 1960s] all my social life was underground gay. It was my own life. I kept it separate from work, where I went on publicity dates with Annette Funicello or Roberta Shore.

—Tommy Kirk

☆ ☆ ☆ ☆

I was caught having sex with a boy at a public school in Burbank. We were both young, and the boy's mother went to Walt Disney....It was toward the end of my contract, and he told me I was in trouble. He advised that I'd better start liking girls and *fast*.

—ex–teen star Tommy Kirk

☆ ☆ ☆ ☆

Graham Chapman [a fellow member of Monty Python] had a coming-out party, and he invited everyone, his friends, associates, all of us. I wasn't entirely clear on what a coming-out party was, but it sounded like fun, and I half-expected there to be debutantes. But Gray really meant *coming out*....He introduced us to his boyfriend and grinningly informed us he was a homosexual...and it was a most jolly party.

—John Cleese

☆ ☆ ☆ ☆

A miserable newspaperwoman wrote something implying that Rock Hudson, Julie [Andrews], and I were a sexual threesome. She also implied that Rock and I had spent a lot of time together in San Francisco leather bars....I walked up to Rock and repeated the story to him, and I loved his response: "How in the hell did she find out so quick?"

—Blake Edwards

☆ ☆ ☆ ☆

There's no way this story [that Neil Simon lost his wife, Marsha Mason, to her] could be true, and I have to believe that anyone

who knows the three of us knows that [although] I'm di-
vorced,...I live alone, am outspoken politically, and have been
very involved with the equal rights movement....

—Joan Hackett

☆ ☆ ☆ ☆

Judy Davis is sexy because she is talented....Catherine Crier on
CNN is sexy because she's a good reporter....Sexy people are
never sexy. They are the least sexy people.

—Sandra Bernhard

☆ ☆ ☆ ☆

Whether I'm gay or not is irrelevant. Whether I slept with
[Sandra Bernhard] or not is irrelevant. I'm perfectly willing to
have people think that I did.

—Madonna

☆ ☆ ☆ ☆

...k. d. lang, who's gorgeous....She looks like Sean [Penn]. I met
her, and I thought, Oh, my God, she's the female version of Sean.
I could fall in love with her.

—Madonna

☆ ☆ ☆ ☆

The Mutt and Jeff of MTV.
  —Mr. Blackwell on Madonna and Sandra Bernhard

☆ ☆ ☆ ☆

These two gals [Madonna and k. d. lang] have been spotted all
over town together at cozy dinners, dancing, and there's even a
report that they were spotted driving around town in Madonna's
Mercedes together. One source said that the two gals are "an
item," while another spy said that Madonna and k. d. lang are
recording a duet together.

—the Hollywood Kids

☆ ☆ ☆ ☆

Now and then I get the impression that blondes not only have
more fun, they're more apt to be bisexual. Judy Holliday,

Marilyn, Madonna, on and on....Maybe blond hair loosens inhibitions.

—Halston

☆ ☆ ☆ ☆

She is my other daughter.
   —Lana Turner on "Josh," the longtime female companion of
               her daughter Cheryl Crane

☆ ☆ ☆ ☆

If Chastity joined the Ku Klux Klan, *then* I would be out of my mind. There are certain things that I think are bad and certain things that I don't really care about. It would be a lot more important to me that Chastity be a good person than what her sexuality is. She is everything I would want her to be—sensitive, smart, talented. But it made a lot better story to say that I was out of my mind about it.
   —Cher commenting on homophobic tabloid stories about her
               daughter's alleged lesbianism

☆ ☆ ☆ ☆

Did you see all those stories about Streisand's son [Jason Gould] holding a wedding ceremony with that handsome male model? I thought it was great that Barbra showed up; she seemed very supportive. But then she said in *Vanity Fair* that she'd be glad for her son if he were happy with a chimp! What kind of a dumb comparison is that? Oh, well, to paraphrase Doris Day, *Gay será, será.*

—Peter Allen

☆ ☆ ☆ ☆

Judy [Garland] attracted gays—gay men. Everyone says her father was bi. At least one of her husbands was gay—I toured with Judy, and I know. I was best man at one of her weddings....What I'm not positive of is whether Judy knew about Peter Allen [being gay]. She stage-managed his marriage to Liza Minnelli—it was Liza's first and Peter's last.

—Johnnie Ray

I don't believe Mickey Rooney. In his memoirs he says he had an affair with Norma Shearer! Why would she stoop so low? He also says that supposedly the reason he never had an affair with Judy was that she'd already had an affair with some female singer and was dubious about her own sexuality. Couldn't it be that she just didn't find Mickey Rooney at all attractive? That makes sense to me!

—Peter Allen

☆ ☆ ☆ ☆

Judy's comeback doing live performances was possible via her legions of gay fans. They didn't care that perhaps she'd lost her looks or wasn't young anymore; they just wanted to see and hear her in person....I was there, the night of April 23, 1961, when she had her historic triumph at Carnegie Hall. It's a date I will never forget.

—Rock Hudson

☆ ☆ ☆ ☆

I never heard rumors about Judy. About [ex-husband] Vincente Minnelli, yes. Often.

—Rock Hudson

☆ ☆ ☆ ☆

Yes, one of Judy's biographers wrote that she was filming *The Pirate* [1948] with Gene Kelly, and Vincente Minnelli directing. That she suspected her leading man and her husband-director of having an affair. A bit difficult to believe—Minnelli was so unlovely....I don't know a thing about Kelly, but I have always heard Minnelli was a deeply closeted chap.

—Peter Allen

☆ ☆ ☆ ☆

Minnelli began as a costumer and an art director. In the thirties, before he came to Hollywood, he was responsible for the whole look of the fabulous stage shows at Radio City Music Hall. Later in life, he declined to discuss those predirectorial days when he'd been a designer. Even so, he was seen around Hollywood wearing bright yellow jackets—quite daring, before the sartorial revolution of the sixties....For some time, Minnelli was very attached to his Japanese valet; don't think there weren't rumors about *that*.

—Halston

☆ ☆ ☆ ☆

The producers and studio chiefs did tend to deprecate directors who began as designers, which very few directors did. M-G-M brought Vincente out here to direct but wouldn't give him an assignment. At length, they assigned him to do *Cabin in the Sky*, an all-colored musical. That was not viewed as a prestige assignment, and his career didn't really take off until he married Judy Garland a few years later....

—George Cukor

☆ ☆ ☆ ☆

He was just a decorator, like Minnelli.
—Billy Wilder on Mitchell Leisen, another director who began as a designer

☆ ☆ ☆ ☆

I got the part of Cesare Borgia in *Bride of Vengeance* because Mitch Leisen, the director, also designed the costumes. Ray Milland refused to do that part because he heard Leisen was going to personally fit each of the men for his codpiece! Ray saw that as a major encroachment on his masculinity. I'd already worked with Mitch, he respected me, so I played opposite Paulette Goddard as [Cesare's sister] Lucrezia Borgia.
—MacDonald Carey

☆ ☆ ☆ ☆

Charles Farrell didn't mind so much being labeled an anti-Semite. But he did mind being called a homosexual.
—Ralph Bellamy, who, with Farrell, founded the Palm Springs Racquet Club

☆ ☆ ☆ ☆

Some of the worst homophobes, in Washington or Hollywood, are closeted homosexuals. Like J. Edgar Hoover, who kept a file on Rock Hudson and informed one of the studios that Hudson would not meet his approval to play an FBI agent in a movie! Or Rock himself, who, like Liberace, didn't leave one penny in his will to help gay rights or to fight AIDS....

—Colin Higgins

☆ ☆ ☆ ☆

These homophobic so-called comics like Eddie Murphy and Andrew Dice Clay and Sam Kinison, I think they're very scared, insecure men. They may be frightened of a part of their personality that possibly they're repressing. I mean, they're obsessed with homosexuality, and that isn't natural for a hetero-sexual. Either you know you're gay, or you know you're not. I think it's the guys who aren't sure that are the most violent, either verbally or physically.

—James Kirkwood

☆ ☆ ☆ ☆

I do this under protest. Sam Kinison is the first pig to ever host a rock-'n'-roll show....I hope in the future the producers will get someone decent, instead of an [bleeped].
—Elton John, presenting an award on a televised music-
awards ceremony that he didn't know would be
cohosted by homophobe Kinnison

☆ ☆ ☆ ☆

George Cukor gave me my big break in this business. He thought I could be a star, and I knew somebody important like him could really help me, so I let him take his pleasure, and it didn't compromise me in the least. Everyone knew he was homosexual; it was no secret.

—Aldo Ray

☆ ☆ ☆ ☆

He [Cukor] wasn't even born in the 1900s. He was the type of gay Jew who would never dream of admitting to anyone that, yes, he was gay and he was Jewish. Above all, he wished to be thought very rich yet very common....

—John Carradine

☆ ☆ ☆ ☆

He was not a happy person.

—Katharine Hepburn on Cukor

☆ ☆ ☆ ☆

I think he was the happiest professional who ever lived in Hollywood.

—writer-director Joseph L. Mankiewicz on Cukor

☆ ☆ ☆ ☆

Mr. Cukor had the most magnificent house in Hollywood and probably directed more classic motion pictures than anyone else. So what if he only got one Academy Award? Living well and leaving behind an endless legacy is a damned good revenge!

—Adela Rogers St. Johns

☆ ☆ ☆ ☆

One of the oddest couples Hollywood or New York had ever seen was the American actress Paulette Goddard and the Mexican painter Frida Kahlo. If one of them had only been blond, they'd have made a perfectly beautiful couple!

—Salvador Dalí

☆ ☆ ☆ ☆

A natural-born honeypot.
—what lesbian actress-coach Constance Collier called bisexual actress Paulette Goddard

☆ ☆ ☆ ☆

Connie [Collier] was one of Kate Hepburn's best friends, but the one she was mad about was Dietrich. Connie pursued Dietrich in the mid-1930s. I don't think she got anywhere, though. With women, Dietrich seemed to prefer being the aggressor.

—Natalie Schafer

☆ ☆ ☆ ☆

Tallulah had more girlfriends than Errol Flynn!

—Patsy Kelly

Tallulah never beat about the bush—she'd gossip about you in *front* of your back!

—Patsy Kelly

☆ ☆ ☆ ☆

I did a movie with Miss Bankhead in England. One day, she wandered into my dressing room, completely nude. I couldn't help staring, and she said, "What's the matter, dahling? Haven't you ever seen a blonde before?"

—Donald Sutherland

☆ ☆ ☆ ☆

[Katharine Hepburn is] a great friend of mine, though I don't see her very often. I think Katie and Garbo have the two most interesting faces I've ever seen in the movies....As a child, I adored women like Norma Talmadge, Pauline Frederick—all the vamps. Not the Pickfords. Oh, Nazimova I adored!

—Tallulah Bankhead

☆ ☆ ☆ ☆

Everyone assumed Alla Nazimova and [director] Charles Bryant were married, but with Alla preferring her women friends, of whom she had a great many, and Bryant being a cold Englishman, I doubt whether they even had an affair, and I am convinced they were not married.

—Sheilah Graham

☆ ☆ ☆ ☆

People remember Alla Nazimova, if at all, for her sprawling house and gardens that were turned into the legendary hotel the Garden of Allah [since demolished, now supplanted by a savings and loan]. But somebody should write a book, *All About Alla,* or something....She introduced Valentino to his two frigid wives, she was Nancy Davis's [Reagan] godmother, she was M-G-M's top-paid star, she was Broadway's biggest draw, she had an affair with Oscar Wilde's niece....She's more interesting than almost any actress from the sound era.

—producer Irene Mayer Selznick, daughter of Louis B. Mayer
and wife of David O. Selznick

The biggest phony in Hollywood, dahling! A lying lesbo, a Polish publicity hound! She showed up at Valentino's funeral and pretended that they'd fallen in love and had been engaged to be married—didn't leave her a cent, dahling! To demonstrate her grief for the cameras, she fainted at the funeral, not just once, but on request. A lousy actress. Had a mustache and couldn't act her way out of a paper bag!

—Tallulah on Pola Negri

☆ ☆ ☆ ☆

How the hell should I know, dahling? He never sucked *my* cock!
—Tallulah's response when asked if her costar Tab Hunter was gay

☆ ☆ ☆ ☆

There were little boys around the house all the time....As far as his sexual (orientation), he has never had a girlfriend, ever!
—La Toya Jackson on brother Michael

☆ ☆ ☆ ☆

You can't go around getting flowers from a fag like that.
—André Agassi to Pete Sampras after Sampras received a good-luck bouquet from tennis fan Elton John

☆ ☆ ☆ ☆

Yeah, I'd like to make movies. Things like *Silence of the Gerbils* with Richard Gere or *Bambi Goes Butch* with Jodie Foster.
—Judy Tenuta

☆ ☆ ☆ ☆

And Mickey Rourke is just so adorable. Dumb, but with some magic....And he and Chris Walken kissed each other goodbye on the lips so tenderly, it looked so gay.
—Andy Warhol

☆ ☆ ☆ ☆

The *National Enquirer* once printed an article that said (gymnast) Mitch Gaylord and I were lovers. Some of my friends asked me if I was upset. I told them not at all.
—Scott Valentine of *Family Ties*

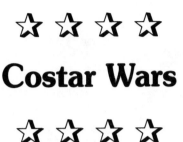

Costar Wars

Kissing Marilyn Monroe was like kissing Hitler!
> —Tony Curtis

✩ ✩ ✩ ✩

Fredric March was able to do a very emotional scene with tears in his eyes and pinch my fanny at the same time.
> —Shelley Winters

✩ ✩ ✩ ✩

Doris Day is a great gal, the best pro I ever worked with. After two films, I had her drinking, smoking, and saying naughty words.
> —Rod Taylor

✩ ✩ ✩ ✩

You were very good in it, Olivia. When you weren't in a scene with me, you managed to keep the audience's attention.
> —Bette Davis to Olivia de Havilland after viewing
> *Hush...Hush, Sweet Charlotte*

✩ ✩ ✩ ✩

He always said that if he hadn't had an accent, he wouldn't have been typecast in pictures. But if he hadn't had an accent, he wouldn't have become a star by being cast as Dracula!
> —Basil Rathbone on Bela Lugosi

179

Beauty and the beast: Bela Lugosi and Helen Chandler

Burt Reynolds has worked with almost every leading lady in Hollywood. He really loathed only two—Raquel Welch and Kathleen Turner. Loni Anderson doesn't count—he married her....

—Sarah Miles, Reynolds's costar in *The Man Who Loved Cat Dancing*

She stole everything but the cameras.

—George Raft on newcomer Mae West

☆ ☆ ☆ ☆

I wouldn't call her a warm personality....Costarring with Greta Garbo does not constitute an introduction.

—Robert Montgomery

☆ ☆ ☆ ☆

[Fred Astaire] used to tell us how Judy Garland was overeating and how it was no wonder she became so huge. Oh, he was a gossip!

—Leslie Caron

☆ ☆ ☆ ☆

My first Oscar nomination was for a dull picture, *Come to the Stable*. With Loretta Young as a nun. I tried to like Miss Young, but she didn't make it easy, pretending to be so wholly holy all the time. Her one big flaw is her two faces.

—Elsa Lanchester

☆ ☆ ☆ ☆

I tell you the truth. I wouldn't even stand next to her [Susan Saint James of *McMillan and Wife*] at a cocktail party!

—Rock Hudson

☆ ☆ ☆ ☆

Betty Grable! She'd murder you. I remember once I got her angry on the set. She stormed over and said, "You know why I'm doing this picture? I thought they said Dan *Duryea!*"

—Dan Dailey

☆ ☆ ☆ ☆

Susan Hayward was an ice queen—very like Grace Kelly that way. Oh, Susan wasn't mean or anything, but when we'd be standing there, ready to shoot our scenes, she was so silent and remote....

—Bob Cummings

On the set with Charlton Heston, a graduate of the Mt. Rushmore school of acting....They were setting up, and we'd been sitting side by side, in silence, some twenty minutes. Finally, I turn to Chuck and say, "You know, I just can't sit next to somebody for nearly a half an hour and not even say hello. He turns to me slowly, very condescending, and says, "Well, I can."

—Edward G. Robinson

☆ ☆ ☆ ☆

I'm appalled at the way other actors work. On *Will Penny,* Charlton Heston, every day at five in the afternoon, would say, "It's cold as hell, let's close this thing down," and go off and have a brandy.

—Joan Hackett

☆ ☆ ☆ ☆

When we costarred in *Becket,* I wanted Larry [Olivier] to be my buddy. But he didn't want to know. He just wasn't interested. I tell you, I felt like a schoolboy with a crush on his teacher. I loved and was not loved. I was terribly hurt.

—Anthony Quinn

☆ ☆ ☆ ☆

I've outlasted everybody, bar none. I was in *The Misfits.* You know it? It was the last picture made by Marilyn Monroe and by Clark Gable....I liked *her*....Lovely child. Terribly insecure. Gable was very insecure. The first time he laid eyes upon you, he decided whether he liked you or not. More, I don't care to say.

—Estelle Winwood

☆ ☆ ☆ ☆

Working with Marilyn Monroe in *The Misfits* nearly gave me a heart attack. I have never been happier when a film ended.

—Clark Gable

☆ ☆ ☆ ☆

I said to Marilyn, "Why can't you get here on time, for fuck's sake?" And she replied, "Oh, do you have that word in England, too?"

—Laurence Olivier

Monroe! I never could understand what it was all about. She was absolutely talentless. To work with her was agony. In the first place, she never was there. You'd wait; five o'clock at night she'd show up on the set.

—Tony Randall

☆ ☆ ☆ ☆

Marilyn was frightened, insecure....During our scenes in *How to Marry a Millionaire,* she'd look at my forehead instead of my eyes....A scene often went to fifteen or more takes, which meant I'd have to be good in all of them, as no one knew which one would be used. Yet I couldn't dislike Marilyn. She had no meanness in her, no bitchery.

—Lauren Bacall

☆ ☆ ☆ ☆

John Wayne, my leading man in *A Lady Takes a Chance,* was late to show his political potential. If I had known then [1943] what I know now, I think I would have shot him dead on the spot.

—Jean Arthur

☆ ☆ ☆ ☆

Bing Crosby and I weren't the types to go around kissing each other. We always had a light jab for each other....One of our stock lines used to be "There's nothing I wouldn't do for Bing, and there's nothing he wouldn't do for me. And that's the way we go through life—doing nothing for each other."

—Bob Hope

☆ ☆ ☆ ☆

At the party for *The Women* at the Trocadero, I was dancing with George Cukor when Ernst Lubitsch fox-trotted by and said, "If you want more close-ups in the picture, never mind your director; you'd better dance with Norma Shearer!" [Shearer, top-billed over Crawford and Russell, was the widow of M-G-M's Irving Thalberg.] So then Norma and I did a turn on the floor.

—Rosalind Russell

☆ ☆ ☆ ☆

Joan Crawford had wanted Claire Trevor for my part in *Johnny Guitar*. Everything was all right until [filming] on location in Arizona. I had a four-page monologue, and because of my stage and radio background, I knew all the lines. We shot it in one take, and the crew applauded. Joan was in her trailer and heard the applause—and that started it. It made Joan mad, and *she* was the star of the picture....

—Mercedes McCambridge

☆ ☆ ☆ ☆

On *Johnny Guitar* we had an actress [McCambridge] who hadn't worked in ten years, an excellent actress but a rabble-rouser....Her delight was to create friction. "Did you hear what *he* said about *you*?" she'd tell me. "And in front of a group of people!" I couldn't believe it....She would finish a scene, walk to the phone on the set, and call one of the columnists to report my "incivilities." I was as civil as I knew how to be.

—Joan Crawford

☆ ☆ ☆ ☆

Poor old rotten-egg Joan. I kept my mouth shut about her for nearly a quarter of a century, but she was a mean, tipsy, powerful, rotten-egg lady. I'm still not going to tell what she did to me. Other people have written some of it, but they don't know it all, and they never will because I am a very nice person and I don't like to talk about the dead even if they were rotten eggs.

—Mercedes McCambridge

☆ ☆ ☆ ☆

There is not enough money in Hollywood to lure me into making another picture with Joan Crawford. And I like money.

—Sterling Hayden

☆ ☆ ☆ ☆

Joan Crawford used continually to knit, whether she was rehearsing or eating, looking at rushes, or doing battle with someone. Oscar Levant asked her, "Do you knit when you fuck?" For days after, there were icebergs on the set of *Humoresque*.

—director Jean Negulesco

Beauty and the beauty: Nils Asther and Joan Crawford

My first film, I enacted an associate of Bette Davis. We were each nominated for an Academy Award; Miss Crawford wasn't....A few years later, I played Miss Davis's father, although I'm thirty years her junior. Working with Bette Davis was very maturing—in both senses of the word!

—Victor Buono [*What Ever Happened to Baby Jane?* and *Hush...Hush, Sweet Charlotte*]

When I made *The Scapegoat* with Alec Guinness, he cut my part into such shreds that my appearance in the final product made no sense at all. This is an actor who plays by himself and unto himself. In this particular picture he plays a dual role, so at least he was able to play with himself.

—Bette Davis

☆ ☆ ☆ ☆

It was sad to see Paul Muni slowly disappear behind his elaborate makeup, his putty noses, his false lips, his beards. One of the few funny things Jack Warner ever said was "Why are we paying him so much money when we can't find him?"

—Bette Davis

☆ ☆ ☆ ☆

Miss [Bette] Davis felt rather sorry for me because I had a small role [in *Dead Ringer*]. If so, it was a waste of her time. I'm more memorable in a small role than many stars in bigger ones. Fans tell me they remember my scenes better than the stars'.

—Estelle Winwood

☆ ☆ ☆ ☆

Miss [Lucille] Ball was very nice to me. Eventually, I heard she was bloody rough on those younger than she was. But she was nice to me. She always liked to see me sitting down. She would lean over and ask me if all was well. I kept assuring her that it was. I think she was afraid of old age, what it might do to her comedy and her looks. She probably looked at me and saw herself—if she were lucky to live as long.

—Estelle Winwood, who lived to 101

☆ ☆ ☆ ☆

On *All I Desire,* I don't recall finding Barbara Stanwyck sympathetic. She was always so popular, and everybody adored her, but I found her a cold person, and she was the only actress in my working experience who ever went home leaving me to do the close-ups with the script girl, which I thought most unprofessional. I was quite surprised. There, that's the only unkind thing that's ever been said about Barbara Stanwyck!

—Maureen O'Sullivan

There was never much of a camaraderie among women stars at M-G-M....I remember when I was in *East Side, West Side* the star was Barbara Stanwyck. I had only one scene with her, but I'll never forget it. Barbara never even looked at me through the scene. Even when we were off-camera, she ignored me. I am convinced her aim was to make things as difficult for me as she could. She succeeded. I was shy and inexperienced, so that was quite a blow.

—Cyd Charisse

☆ ☆ ☆ ☆

George Raft and Gary Cooper once played a scene in front of a cigar store, and it looked like the wooden Indian was overacting.

—George Burns

☆ ☆ ☆ ☆

I don't understand this Method stuff. I remember Laurence Olivier asking Dustin Hoffman why he stayed up all night. Dustin, looking really beat, really bad, said it was to get into the scene being filmed that day, in which he was supposed to have been up all night. Olivier said, "My boy, if you'd learn how to act you wouldn't have to stay up all night."

—Robert Mitchum

☆ ☆ ☆ ☆

Ginger [Rogers] drove Fred [Astaire] crazy with her dresses. There was the molting one with all the feathers in *Top Hat*. And for the "Let's Face the Music and Dance" number in *Follow the Fleet*, she wore a beaded gown that must've weighed fifty pounds! And when she turned around one time, her long, beaded sleeve knocked Fred clear across the room!

—choreographer Hermes Pan

☆ ☆ ☆ ☆

Astaire knew he was a talent, and he knew he was plain. He knew, besides, that he was aging, and he once vetoed a gown that Cyd Charisse would have worn [in *Silk Stockings*] because she looked too beautiful in it. And youthful. His excuse was that it was "wrong" for their dance number, but the truth was that the gown made her look too good.

—Ann Miller

I did a movie with Bogart, *Sabrina*. It proved to me that in Hollywood, stars don't just grow old, they grow paranoid. Bogey was suspicious of my and Audrey Hepburn's every move. Why? We were younger than him.

—William Holden

☆ ☆ ☆ ☆

My costar status in *Cleopatra* was jeopardized by the overly publicized affair between Elizabeth Taylor and Richard Burton. She did get top billing, so I facetiously suggested billing the picture "Elizabeth Taylor in *Heat*," and it took the Fox executives a while to realize that I wasn't really serious.

—Rex Harrison

☆ ☆ ☆ ☆

Rex was nicer to his leading ladies than his wives. They got the pleasant public face. The wives get the cold reality. If we hadn't been shackled together, he'd have flirted with me on the set, just for appearances, for his credentials—those get more important as a man gets older. Rex was always afraid of being past it.

—ex-wife and ex-costar Rachel Roberts

☆ ☆ ☆ ☆

[Truman Capote]: Like Katharine Hepburn—arrogant. But not half so pretty, or thin. Underneath, he wants to be liked. But he's got the warmth of an alligator.... The press was fawning over him. Because it's his first motion picture [*Murder by Death*], I suppose. It may be his last. He's not a fine actor; he plays himself, and you can get that on television for free.

—Estelle Winwood

☆ ☆ ☆ ☆

Day after day [on the set of *Mary of Scotland*], Katharine Hepburn kept saying she really wanted to play *both* Mary and Queen Elizabeth [played by Florence Eldridge]. We all got tired of hearing it. So one day I told Kate, "If you played both parts, how would you know which queen to upstage?" She walked off the set and didn't speak to me for twenty years.

—John Carradine

How affected can you be in the middle of Africa? Katharine Hepburn [filming *The African Queen*] used to say that everything was "divine." The goddamn stinking natives were "divine." "Oh, what a *divine* native!" she'd say. "Oh, what a *divine* pile of manure!"

—Humphrey Bogart

☆ ☆ ☆ ☆

Of all the people I performed with, I got to know Cary Grant least of all. He is a completely private person, totally reserved, and there is no way into him.... Distant. Very distant.

—Doris Day

☆ ☆ ☆ ☆

There were prima donnas in the old days as well. I worked with Orson Welles, who himself repeated to me the story someone had once said about him: "There but for the grace of God goes God." By that point, I think Welles had ceased caring about art and settled into a celebrity attitude. Which of course could be said of most of us who agreed to participate in *Casino Royale.*

—David Niven

☆ ☆ ☆ ☆

Welles's influence on *Jane Eyre?* You cannot battle an elephant. Orson was such a big man in every way that no one could stand up to him. On the first day, we were all called on the set at one o'clock. No Welles. At four o'clock, he strode in, followed by his agent, a dwarf, his valet, and a whole entourage. Approaching, us, he proclaimed, "All right, everybody, turn to page eight." And we did—though he wasn't even the director!

—Joan Fontaine

☆ ☆ ☆ ☆

Everybody in town has had Yvonne De Carlo!

—Tony Curtis

☆ ☆ ☆ ☆

Everybody in Hollywood has had Tony Curtis!

—Yvonne De Carlo

It's like being hit over the head with a Valentine's card every day.
—Christopher Plummer on working with Julie Andrews in
The Sound of Music

☆ ☆ ☆ ☆

Fred Astaire is so diplomatic. He'll never say, though he's always asked, which of his dancing ladies was his favorite partner. If you ask me, he preferred the solo turns.

—Vera-Ellen

☆ ☆ ☆ ☆

I felt a little funny when we were going to do the bed scene, all four of us, in *Bob and Carol and Ted and Alice*. I'm open to suggestions, I'm no prude, but four is a crowd in *my* book. Fortunately, Dyan Cannon was there. The thought of another woman being in there in the bed helped get me through it. It's not like it sounds. It's just that I don't think I could have done it if it had been me and three men.

—Natalie Wood

☆ ☆ ☆ ☆

When we did *The Fan*, I didn't get to meet Lauren Bacall till toward the end of shooting. Didn't work with her that much, but it was very negative. She was unfriendly and treated me like the character I was playing—a lethal fan.

—Michael Biehn

☆ ☆ ☆ ☆

I was never so scared in my life. And I was in the war!
—John Mills on working with Bette Davis

☆ ☆ ☆ ☆

She ought to know about close-ups. Jesus, she was around when they invented them! The bitch has been around forever, you know!
—Bette Davis's reaction when told how wonderful Lillian Gish had been in a close-up in *The Whales of August*

That face! Have you ever seen such a tragic face? Poor woman. How she must be suffering! I don't think it's right to judge a person like that. We must bear and forbear.

—Lillian Gish on Bette Davis

☆ ☆ ☆ ☆

[Bette Davis] started by snapping at me the first day. I said, "Good morning," and she looked right through me. Later, when the cast gathered for introductions, our eyes met, and I waved. "What's that mean?" she snapped. "I was saying good morning," I answered. "You already did that!" she snapped back.

—Helen Hayes re *Murder with Mirrors,*
costarring John Mills

☆ ☆ ☆ ☆

While Bette Davis has indeed always been one of my idols, she did make mincemeat out of poor Lillian when they made *The Whales of August,* a lovely picture. Lillian swears she'll never act again. So first she drove *me* from the screen, now she's driven Lillian. She's making a clean sweep of everyone our age!

—Helen Hayes

☆ ☆ ☆ ☆

Doris Day was not only the eternal virgin, she was the eternal Pollyanna! She didn't care for reality or for people all that much, and she found her ideal philosophy and atmosphere in Christian Science and in dogs. She as much as informed the press that she loved her dogs more than she loved her only child. Milk shakes and mutts—those were the two loves of her life when I worked with her. I don't say "when I knew her," because I didn't really get to know her, though we did have a lot of laughs, lotsa giggles. I don't think even *she* knows the real Doris Day.

—Rock Hudson

☆ ☆ ☆ ☆

I played with Nick Adams, and I acted with Nick Adams [in *Pillow Talk*]. Short guy—big man on campus....

—Rock Hudson

He ain't heavy...: Doris Day, Nick Adams, and Rock Hudson

☆ ☆ ☆ ☆

Ron Howard? Did I ever work with Ron Howard? I'm not sure.
I've done so much television....I read this quote from Ron
Howard. He said, "I'm kind of dull." *Kind* of?...I worked with
Kaye Ballard [on TV's *The Mothers-in-Law*]. She called me
stupid, but there's some names I could call her, only not in print.
The producer was Desi Arnaz—what a lech! Anything female
within thirteen to thirty, he'd go after.

—Roger C. Carmel

☆ ☆ ☆ ☆

Irene Dunne was a law unto herself when she was still making
pictures. Reminded me of a martini, actually—you know, an ice
cube with a hole in it.

—Rex Harrison

Vanessa Redgrave gets on my tits!
>—Trevor Howard using a British expression

☆ ☆ ☆ ☆

...Wasn't Dennis Hooper [*sic*] in *Easy Rider*? I hated that movie.
I wouldn't work with any of the miscreants in it—never have,
never will!
>—John Wayne, who did work with Hopper
>in *The Sons of Katie Elder*

☆ ☆ ☆ ☆

He doesn't get along with anyone. He's a miserably unhappy
man, unhappy that he hasn't become a Hollywood-type star.
Most of us in this country become actors for the love of acting,
not for hoke and glory.
>—Trevor Howard on fellow Brit Anthony Hopkins

☆ ☆ ☆ ☆

When Larry [Olivier] did *Private Lives*, nobody could have
imagined that he would become a leading light of the theater or
anywhere else outside the bedroom. He was a beautiful creature
with lots and lots of ambition.When he failed to take Hollywood
by storm, he focused on the stage and decided that continually
changing masks would make clear how very talented he was.
>—Noel Coward

☆ ☆ ☆ ☆

Maggie Smith was playing [in *The Prime of Miss Jean Brodie*] a
character I was supposed to dislike. She duly obliged. The
affectations and idiosyncrasies notwithstanding, she embodied
some of the worst traits of the English, such as smugness and a
superior air. Unlike Gordon Jackson, who is Scottish, she didn't
share any camaraderie with the crew. During location filming in
Scotland, Miss Smith did not endear herself to the locals. To put
it discreetly, they found her a wee bit "refined" for their tastes.
>—Celia Johnson

☆ ☆ ☆ ☆

Thespians: Laurence Olivier and Noel Coward

James Arness was great in *Gunsmoke,* and we had chemistry. But he's not someone I'd care to spend much time with. Like most actors, he insists on being the center of attention, is insecure, and requires a constant flow of praise. He's just contrary. He likes to start fights and also likes to be the one to end them. That is not my cup of tea.

—Amanda Blake

Charlton Heston costarred with me [in *The Agony and the Ecstasy*....He was in ecstasy over getting to play someone like Michelangelo, and I was in agony over his vanity, his ego, the delays....He treated me as a supporting actor in spite of it being the story of two titans and their relationship. I wasn't playing one of Michelangelo's boyfriends, I was the pope, for heaven's sake!

—Rex Harrison

☆ ☆ ☆ ☆

When we did *Golden Earrings,* I played a gypsy....Ray Milland got top billing, yet he resented me because only a few years earlier, I would have got top billing. Without putting up a fight, as he had to....Ray Milland was not careful of his personal hygiene—he stank! I decided to outdo him. I didn't take any baths during filming, and he had to do love scenes with me, and sometimes I flubbed a line, and the director [Mitchell Leisen] made Ray Milland more nervous and agitated. By the time we finished the picture, I left my top-billed costar a nervous wreck!
Now I see that Ray Milland has lost all his hair. So there!

—Marlene Dietrich

☆ ☆ ☆ ☆

Jane Wyman has had the same girlish hairdo for decades. The one with the bangs. Or as they call her in England, "the girl with the fringe." But she's not a girl anymore, and it's beginning to look a little grisly....

—Rock Hudson

☆ ☆ ☆ ☆

Judith Anderson is a genuinely spooky lady. She didn't have to act very hard for the part of Mrs. Danvers [in *Rebecca*]. Joan Fontaine said she was naturally eerie! When I did *Laura,* the first day we worked together, Miss Anderson was rather charming. I concluded that Joan was wrong about her. However, all it was was a one-day best behavior. From the second day, I learned that Judith Anderson was in a permanent snit about something or other.

—Gene Tierney

☆ ☆ ☆ ☆

Donna Reed [in *From Here To Eternity*] was sort of a cold fish. Personally, I never was able to warm to her. Years after, she earned her own star in *The Donna Reed Show* on television. That's when I saw that she *is* a good actress, because she's so warm and likable on her program. It appears as if she's just being her natural self, but it ain't so! She's acting.

—Montgomery Clift

☆ ☆ ☆ ☆

My film *Rich and Famous* is a contemporary female "buddy" movie as well as a remake of *Old Acquaintance*, which starred Bette Davis and Miriam Hopkins, who hated each other on and off the set. Jackie Bisset and Candice Bergen don't hate each other, but there was definitely some competition between them. Miss Bergen ran with her more flamboyant role. Insiders are saying that she steals the picture right from under Miss Bisset, that comedy is her forte. Both women are on a par as beauties, but it must rankle Candice to have Jackie billed first—a reflection of the fact that Jackie hasn't had as many flops as Candice has.

Their competitiveness may also stem from Jackie having a production participation in *Rich and Famous* and Candy being the daughter of a famous entertainer [Edgar Bergen]. Children of the rich and famous usually have something to prove....

—George Cukor

☆ ☆ ☆ ☆

In the late 1950s I starred in a flick called *I Married a Monster from Outer Space*. Even so, it took me another decade to quit films [and become a bestselling novelist]. One of my cohorts in that particular space epic was an actor named Ty Hardin. A Clint Eastwood clone in looks and acting. If Hardin had become famous first, you'd never have heard of Eastwood, instead of the other way 'round....Harding explained that his original name was Orson Hungerford, but he had to change it because the movie bigwigs didn't like "Orson," as in Welles, and you couldn't have "hunger" in Hollywood, especially on a marquee!

Not very long ago, I asked an associate, "What ever happened to Ty Hardin?" He became a minister! Have you noticed how many nonstar actors become preachers? It permits them to keep overacting, without the guilt. Instead, they can lay the guilt on everyone else.

My personal opinion is, never trust any ex-actor who becomes a preacher or a politician. Let them find honest work instead.
—Tom Tryon

☆ ☆ ☆ ☆

Before I ever worked with Faye Dunaway, I admired her cheekbones. After all, she was a fashion model, wasn't she? Now I can only admire her cheek. And she *acts* like a fashion model!
—Bette Davis

☆ ☆ ☆ ☆

Faye Dunaway is the most unprofessional actress I ever worked with, and that includes Miriam Hopkins, even!
—Bette Davis

☆ ☆ ☆ ☆

Fred Astaire is a wonderful dancer. That's his one talent. He's not an outstanding actor, nor a singer, nor a dashing romantic figure, nor all that amiable. Fred is a pro. He also thinks he's Terpsichore's gift to the world.
—Jack Buchanan

☆ ☆ ☆ ☆

They partnered me with the most splendid actresses—Garbo, Crawford, Stanwyck....Garbo was sweet and shy, terrified of men, comfortable only among a few women. Barbara Stanwyck didn't like men; she had contempt for most everybody. Joan Crawford had contempt for herself, an insecure, frightened woman. They made up that very true, famous saying about Crawford—she excelled at suffering in mink.
—Nils Asther

☆ ☆ ☆ ☆

Laurence Harvey. I do not like to speak ill of the dead or the ill-mannered. But without doubt or exaggeration, he was the most conceited of all the actors with whom I played. *Room at the Top* was the film which brought me to the Academy Award, and it was the film which brought upon me Laurence Harvey. He did not act as if he needed any costars. He treated me as if I were invisible. So I must have won the Oscar for doing nothing, you see. Laurence Harvey acted each line of dialogue as if it were a monologue.

—Simone Signoret

☆ ☆ ☆ ☆

At Warner Brothers, I acted with Errol Flynn. *I* acted....At one point, Jack Warner wanted to loan me out to play Scarlett O'Hara in *Gone With the Wind*, with Flynn as Rhett Butler. I was *torn*, because I wanted to play her, naturally, but not with *him*. He couldn't have carried it off, so regretfully I declined. Then they went and cast Clark Gable, and *he* wasn't much more of an actor, so it finally dawned on me that unlike Scarlett, Rhett was an actor-proof part!

—Bette Davis

☆ ☆ ☆ ☆

Burt Lancaster advised me against doing *Hazel*. "Don't do television," he warned. "It'll ruin you!" Burt is a doll and a heck of an actor, but I'm glad I didn't follow his advice. Everybody under forty knows me better from *Hazel*, not from my movies!

—Shirley Booth

☆ ☆ ☆ ☆

Hated her. She talked like a truck driver.

—Tommy Kirk on Jane Wyman

☆ ☆ ☆ ☆

Bitch!

—Tommy Kirk on Elsa Lanchester

☆ ☆ ☆ ☆

In 1965, I'd signed a contract for *The Sons of Katie Elder* with John Wayne, but a week before shooting I went to a Hollywood party that the vice squad busted because of marijuana. I was handcuffed, and photos of me got in the papers with headlines like "Ex-Disney Child Star Arrested for Pot!" So Wayne and the producers fired me.

—Tommy Kirk

☆ ☆ ☆ ☆

I was there [on *Hollywood Squares*] the day the producers fired Paul Lynde. He got so sloshed during the taping that he got up from his square, walked over to the contestants, and started screaming obscenities at them. Then he tried to strangle one of them! Somewhere in Iowa there are two folks who have *never* forgotten their trip to Hollywood!

—Carol Lynley

☆ ☆ ☆ ☆

Paul Lynde was a latter-day Franklin Pangborn, crossed with a hint of Eve Arden. He was priceless, a camp one-of-a-kind. I recall a *Hollywood Squares* episode where he was asked if the recently deceased Smokey the Bear had left a widow. Paul said, "Let's just say that at the services, they had to sedate Ranger Bob."

—Cesar Romero

☆ ☆ ☆ ☆

Vivian [Vance] and I were inseparable. When she was married to Phil Ober, she—God, that man!…He was a terrible man. He used to beat her up. Loved to embarrass her. I told her year after year to get rid of the guy, but if Viv was one thing, it was loyal.…Then she came to work with a shiner. I told her, "If you don't divorce him, I will." She did.

—Lucille Ball

☆ ☆ ☆ ☆

Josephine Baker. We were on Broadway together in 1935. They called her the no-clothes horse. That was in France. On Broadway, brother, she had clothes!

—Bob Hope

☆ ☆ ☆ ☆

In *The Rains of Ranchipur,* Richard Burton...had a bloated self-image. The rest of us joked about his ego, and someone even advised wardrobe to make him bigger turbans. He strongly resisted Jean Negulesco's efforts to help him deliver a good performance. "You're supposed to be an Indian," Negulesco would tell him. "I'm *not* an Indian," Burton would reply loftily. Yet he spent a good deal of time in his dressing room entertaining our dusky little extras, for whom he seemed to have developed a great fondness. For someone who didn't want to play an Indian, he did seem to enjoy playing *with* them.

—Lana Turner

☆ ☆ ☆ ☆

Michael Landon and I didn't know from horses. What do two nice Jewish boys know about riding? Especially me, since I was older. But image is everything, and *Bonanza* made us champion riders in the public eye. At times, our being stereotyped and confined to the western range did cause irritation. We all chafed at the bit, even Dan Blocker. We would joke about getting together and going out on tour in something extremely urbane, like a Noel Coward drawing-room comedy.

—Lorne Greene

☆ ☆ ☆ ☆

Vivian Vance gives me a pain.

—William Frawley

☆ ☆ ☆ ☆

Bill Frawley *is* Fred Mertz. Even more so. He's just as tight, but even crabbier, and he's also tight in the other sense of the word, though never on the set. He made a vow to Desi Arnaz that his drinking would never interfere with *I Love Lucy.*

—Vivian Vance

☆ ☆ ☆ ☆

Bill took a dislike to Viv when he overheard her say that she was too young to play his wife. Or, more precisely, that he was too old to play her husband.

—Lucille Ball

Bill and Vivian never got along. He wouldn't speak to her if he could help it, except in character as Fred. Vivian was very offended by this, until gradually she saw that Bill isn't that crazy about anybody. I'm the only one he really likes.

—Desi Arnaz

☆ ☆ ☆ ☆

Bill sometimes called Viv a "bitch," and Desi "the Cuban heel." God knows what he called me behind my back....

—Lucille Ball

☆ ☆ ☆ ☆

I loved working with Gale Gordon in my other series [plural]. I'd originally suggested him to play Fred Mertz....We all loved the late Bill Frawley, but he wasn't as pleasant to work with as Gale. Gale made our shows together a happy experience. He's a sweetheart!

—Lucille Ball

☆ ☆ ☆ ☆

After all those volatile personalities I encountered in motion pictures, the cast of *Our Miss Brooks* was a dream. We all got along swimmingly. The only one to display any temperament now and then was [Minerva] the cat.

—Eve Arden

☆ ☆ ☆ ☆

Eve [Arden] worked with me twice. I wish she had been given an Academy Award for *Mildred Pierce,* as I was. She deserved one, too....I'm eternally grateful to Eve, for it's thanks to her I was able to adopt my first children. Eve had adopted, and when I told her how desperately I wanted children, she informed me how to go about having children of my own.

—Joan Crawford

☆ ☆ ☆ ☆

Miss Crawford was quite a haughty lady. Perhaps by that time in her life, making *Autumn Leaves,* she was entitled. She was trying to hold on to her dignity, playing a woman in love with a younger man [Cliff Robertson]. She was never rude, but she had a most condescending attitude toward everyone but her director and leading man. She was the queen, and we were the serfs.

—Lorne Greene

☆ ☆ ☆ ☆

I didn't work with Clark Gable or Cary Grant. In part because we were at different studios. Gable didn't like strong females, and Grant was mostly in light comedies. Besides which, he needed willowy or boyish girls like Katharine Hepburn to make him look what they now call macho. If I'd costarred with Grant or if Crawford had, we'd have eaten him for breakfast!

—Bette Davis

☆ ☆ ☆ ☆

Why am I so good at playing bitches? I think it's because I'm not a bitch. Maybe that's why Miss Crawford always plays ladies.

—Bette Davis

☆ ☆ ☆ ☆

I was in Cary Grant's last movie, *Walk, Don't Run*. He's a nice enough man, and when he's not preoccupied with himself, he can be very charming. But the suave Cary Grant we've all witnessed at the movies and the man in real life are two different people....He's not as reserved as most English actors, probably because he's been here so long. He does have a sense of humor; he was fun. We had to wear walking shorts, and he kept complimenting me on my legs, though *he* has very good legs for his age....It's too bad he retired from the movies; I guess he got tired of acting.

—Jim Hutton

☆ ☆ ☆ ☆

When we commenced *On a Clear Day You Can See Forever,* I had the mistaken impression that I was the costar. I was Miss Streisand's first leading man who can sing, even though this was her third musical. And I thought she was my leading lady, a partner. I doubt I will choose to work again in Hollywood....

—Yves Montand

Working with Barbra Streisand is pretty stressful. It's like sitting down to a picnic in the middle of a freeway.
—Kris Kristofferson

☆ ☆ ☆ ☆

Why would I refuse to work with Barbra a second time? The pay is good, and she likes to surround herself with good-looking blonds.
—Ryan O'Neal

☆ ☆ ☆ ☆

Barbra Streisand has as much talent as a butterfly's fart.
—Walter Matthau

☆ ☆ ☆ ☆

I'm the only man who was top-billed over Barbra Streisand. I got first place, but she got $4 million despite it being a much smaller role....Wouldn't you know, it was a flop and almost nobody saw it!
—Gene Hackman, *All Night Long*

☆ ☆ ☆ ☆

She's certifiable!
—Jack Nicholson on Faye Dunaway, *Chinatown*

☆ ☆ ☆ ☆

It's a stretch for him to play someone not quite as boring as he tends to be.
—Ted Knight on Gavin MacLeod, *The Mary Tyler Moore Show*

☆ ☆ ☆ ☆

Bob Hope—his middle name is Money. That's what he loves best.
—Jerry Colonna

☆ ☆ ☆ ☆

Angela Lansbury. She's very nice. That's "ice" with an "n" in front of it....
—Keenan Wynn

I'm in love with Julie Andrews, yes. There's nothing I wouldn't say to her face—both of them.

—Rock Hudson

☆ ☆ ☆ ☆

Shelley Winters is very outspoken. But not by many.

—Ed Wynn

☆ ☆ ☆ ☆

[Orson Welles] can write, direct, produce, even act.

—Ray Milland

☆ ☆ ☆ ☆

Yes, he (Welles) is a perpetual notion machine.

—Marlene Dietrich

☆ ☆ ☆ ☆

Her body has gone to her head.

—Barbara Stanwyck on Marilyn Monroe

☆ ☆ ☆ ☆

With Fox behind her, Miss Monroe will become a big star.

—Darryl F. Zanuck, Fox chief

☆ ☆ ☆ ☆

She won't become a big star because of what's *behind* her.

—George Jessel on Marilyn Monroe

☆ ☆ ☆ ☆

Judy Holliday went in to audition for Harry Cohn, the head of Columbia. He began making advances, but Judy nipped it in the bud. She reached inside her blouse, retrieved her falsies, and said, "Here's what you're after."

—Ruth Gordon

☆ ☆ ☆ ☆

Judy Garland and her fellow Gumm sisters opened for me in [vaudeville in] Chicago in 1931. She was Frances Gumm then. I took one look at her, and she resembled a piglet, with her little turned-up nose. Then I took a listen, and she sang like a jewel. I took an interest in the act. I suggested a new name, something cheerful and festive, like the Garland Sisters. That way, their name couldn't be misspelled like in Chicago, where they were billed as the Glum Sisters.

—George Jessel

☆ ☆ ☆ ☆

[Louis B.] Mayer treated Judy abominably. She was the lowest-paid star in *The Wizard of Oz*. Only Toto got paid less.

—James Mason

☆ ☆ ☆ ☆

Shooting on location isn't the simplest. In Utah, for *The Electric Horseman*, a simple kissing scene with Bob Redford went through almost fifty takes. We started one morning and didn't finish until late the next day!
  —Jane Fonda [To cover the kiss from every angle, more
    than seventy-five hundred feet of film was shot, for a
    sequence lasting twenty seconds in the movie. Their
    kiss cost an estimated $280,000. The cost accountant
    complained, "It would have been cheaper if Redford
                    had kissed the horse."]

☆ ☆ ☆ ☆

Richard Gere? Absolutely no comment!...It takes a long time to recover from *An Officer and a Gentleman*....I'm embarrassed about it. I'm physically wounded from it.

—Debra Winger

☆ ☆ ☆ ☆

Joy in the Morning [1965] was a grim experience. The leading lady [Yvette Mimieux] was a blonde who was accustomed to having her costars flirt back, and maybe then some. When the leading man [Richard Chamberlain] didn't, she proceeded to tell anyone she could that he was homosexual, thus attempting to wreck his career.

—Arthur Kennedy

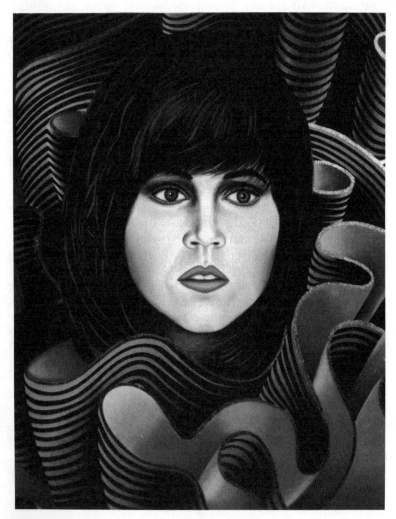

Fonda Jane? (portrait by Sue Kutosh)

☆ ☆ ☆ ☆

Not unless I have to. We have absolutely nothing in common. I think he's a bit of a sad character.
—Cher re her ex-husband and costar Sonny Bono, whom she seldom speaks to

I still have Michael York's nasal voice ringing in my ears....
—Marty Feldman, after *The Last Remake of Beau Geste*

☆ ☆ ☆ ☆

I suppose the chap has rather a decorative quality.... He enacted Jacqueline Bisset's husband—he's a kind of boy version of Bisset, though, isn't he?
—Colin Blakely on Michael York, *Murder on the Orient Express*

☆ ☆ ☆ ☆

Debbie Reynolds played my daughter in *The Pleasure of His Company*. Gary Merrill played my husband. Fred Astaire was my ex-husband. I must say, it came together very beautifully on the screen, a tribute to everyone's professionalism and talent. But with a family like that, I'd sooner become a nun! And I'm Jewish!
—Lilli Palmer

☆ ☆ ☆ ☆

I am big rock star in Japan. In England, David Bowie is big rock star. In *Merry Christmas, Mr. Lawrence* I have to kiss David Bowie on [the] lips, but he is acting, so he does not appreciate this gesture.... When he is not acting, David Bowie is also cold, keeping to himself. He thinks he is the only star.
—Ryuichi Sakamoto

☆ ☆ ☆ ☆

Mr. [Boris] Karloff—always *so* dignified.... In *Frankenstein* he spoke no lines. That is why when they offered it to me, I said, "No. I am a trained actor. I am trained to speak. If I do not speak lines, it is not acting." Then Mr. Karloff accepted to take the part of the monster.
—Bela Lugosi

☆ ☆ ☆ ☆

Charlotte Rampling, but I pronounce it Charlotte Tramp-ling, and nobody ever notices I'm describing the role she always plays.
—James Mason

☆ ☆ ☆ ☆

Richard Harris makes me look sober!

—Richard Burton

☆ ☆ ☆ ☆

I had it in my contract that if [W. C.] Fields got drunk on the set, I stopped everything and had the guy ejected from the lot. It was a pleasure pouring him outta there....

—Mae West

☆ ☆ ☆ ☆

I caught myself staring at Yul Brynner's naked head several times during *Anastasia*. Now I know why; I didn't know then— we were all so much younger, more naive. His head is a phallic symbol!

—Martita Hunt

☆ ☆ ☆ ☆

Jayne Mansfield couldn't act her way out of a paper condom!

—Dan Dailey

☆ ☆ ☆ ☆

Dahling, the main reason I accepted to be in *The Devil and the Deep* was to fuck that divine Gary Cooper!

—Tallulah Bankhead

☆ ☆ ☆ ☆

Carmen Miranda's lack of underwear was causing a lot of friction, to put it mildly. It got out to the public that Carmen felt restricted by panties and didn't wear them. The ladies' clubs and organizations, which were very powerful then, got wind of this and tried to boycott her pictures. It didn't matter to them that nobody ever *saw* that she didn't wear underwear; they just wanted to rest assured in the knowledge that under all that colorful costuming, she was wearing panties and keeping the movies safe for democracy.

—John Payne

I never was turned on by pretty boys. If you want to hear something ridiculous, I was more attracted [on *Paint Your Wagon*] to Lee Marvin than Clint Eastwood. Lee has a sexier singing voice, too....His stubble also looks sexier!

—Jean Seberg

☆ ☆ ☆ ☆

I didn't enjoy working with Rock Hudson. He was a shallow little boy who may have grown tall but never grew up. Self-centered and spoiled, he could never communicate on any level that did not relate to himself.

—Martha Hyer

☆ ☆ ☆ ☆

Rock Hudson's all right. He's a man's man and not a bad actor at all....

—John Wayne

☆ ☆ ☆ ☆

Jennifer Jones was the Meryl Streep of her day. She transformed herself from film to film, varying her type and appearance. She was well-respected but not overly popular....Hollywood prefers a performer to stay the same. Being recognizable, regardless of what one's doing or who one's playing, is the key to movie popularity. Audiences have matured since that time, and now somebody like Meryl Streep is hailed for her diversity. Again, though, she is not major box office—unless she's in a soppy love story with Robert Redford....Meryl Streep is, to me, today's Jennifer Jones.

—Laurence Olivier

☆ ☆ ☆ ☆

I never forget the Sophia Loren of the early days, in Italy. But as she has grown into more of a lady, she is less of a comedienne. *Che peccato* [What a pity.]

—Vittorio De Sica

Patty Duke's behavior during *Me, Natalie* was most erratic. I didn't know what to make of it. I thought she was a Method actress. Afterwards someone informed me she was merely a manic-depressive.

—Elsa Lanchester

☆ ☆ ☆ ☆

For years, Miss [Bette] Davis has been quoting a piece of advice she says Charles [Laughton] gave her: "Never dare not to hang yourself." It sounds like Charles, but I've yet to see evidence that he or Miss Davis has acted on it. . . . Something to look forward to, I suppose.

—Elsa Lanchester

☆ ☆ ☆ ☆

She's just a major, major comedienne in every way. She moves funny, she ad-libs funny, she sings, she dances, she's hilarious.
—Woody Allen on Diane Keaton

☆ ☆ ☆ ☆

Having co-starred with Clint Eastwood [in *Where Eagles Dare*], I cannot quite say that it was a thespic experience on the order of Lunt and Fontanne acting together.

—Richard Burton

☆ ☆ ☆ ☆

They call Cantinflas the Mexican Chaplin, and in silent pictures he might have been an international star, like Charlie. But Cantinflas doesn't translate well. . . . Some years after we worked together [in *Around the World in Eighty Days*], he asked me why Hollywood had virtually ignored him—England too. I really couldn't answer the man. How could I tell him that he's only funny in Spanish?

—David Niven

☆ ☆ ☆ ☆

I worked with Jane fonda in an epic called *Walk on the Wild Side* in the early '60s. I found her to be cold and easily dominated by

Cantinflas: The Mexican Chaplin

men. Not very sympathetic to women. As the years wore on, she got this reputation for being a feminist, but she seems always to be in the shadow of a man—her father or husband, a director, whoever. It's peculiar, because few would describe me as a feminist, yet I think I'm far more independent than she is! I think the media loves a label, and so I'll forever be Eve....

—*All About Eve* star Anne Baxter

(In *Philadelphia*) I'm in love with Antonio Banderas, so I'm the envy of millions of men and women.

—Tom Hanks

☆ ☆ ☆ ☆

(Tina Louise) arrived from New York under the impression it (*Gilligan's Island*) was her series—though with fourth-billing, how she believed that is beyond me...

—Bob "Gilligan" Denver

☆ ☆ ☆ ☆

Robin Williams plays a woman (in *Mrs. Doubtfire*)....Dustin Hoffman played a woman his own age. That's a much bigger challenge. Any guy can play an old lady with a huge chin.

—*Tootsie* costar George Gaynes

☆ ☆ ☆ ☆

Directors' Cuts

☆ ☆ ☆ ☆

She has breasts of granite and a mind like a Gruyere cheese.
—Billy Wilder on Marilyn Monroe

☆ ☆ ☆ ☆

Directing Marilyn Monroe was like directing Lassie. You needed fourteen takes to get one right.
—Otto Preminger

☆ ☆ ☆ ☆

You're too little and too fat, but I might give you a job.
—D. W. Griffith upon meeting Mary Pickford

☆ ☆ ☆ ☆

As a beauty, Dolores Del Rio is in a class with Garbo. Then she opens her mouth and becomes Minnie Mouse.
—John Ford

☆ ☆ ☆ ☆

I've directed some pretty tough customers, John Wayne, Clint Eastwood, and Ronald Reagan among them. But the toughest star I ever directed, in a film titled *Jinxed*, was Bette Midler.
—Don Siegel

When I directed *Tom Jones,* Edith Evans asked me, "I don't look seventy, do I? Now be honest." I replied, "No, love, you don't. Not anymore."

—Tony Richardson

☆ ☆ ☆ ☆

Barbra Streisand's mother once scolded me for not picking her daughter to star in my film *Saint Joan.* I chose another un-

Sir Anthony Asquith directs Dame Edith Evans

known, Jean Seberg. So I told the lady, "Look at Jean Seberg's career. You should *thank* me for not picking your Barbra."
—Otto Preminger

☆ ☆ ☆ ☆

Ray Milland did not deserve an Oscar, but *The Lost Weekend* was the first picture to tackle alcoholism. Tremendous impact. In the same role, W. C. Fields would have won.
—John Huston

☆ ☆ ☆ ☆

I gave Anthony Perkins his first big break. But don't blame me—that's Hollywood, folks!
—George Cukor

☆ ☆ ☆ ☆

A not very happy man, W. C. Fields, but a great comedian. It was *David Copperfield,* and some of the people there got a kick when Fields would bad-mouth the juvenile lead, Freddie Bartholomew. He called him a sissy, and worse. Behind his back; I presume Fields never told him to his face....He could get away with it, however.
—George Cukor

☆ ☆ ☆ ☆

I introduced Kate Hepburn to the screen....At the end of shooting of *A Bill of Divorcement,* Kate had had it with John Barrymore [who had exposed himself to her]. To his face, she told him, "Thank goodness I don't have to act with you anymore." He answered, "I didn't know you ever had, darling."
—George Cukor

☆ ☆ ☆ ☆

Kim Novak was so darned serious on *Vertigo.* She came up to Hitchcock and said, "About the next scene. I'd like to go over it with you because I'm not sure of the reason for the motivation that I have in dealing with the problem that I have...." And Hitchcock just looked at her and said, "Kim, it's only a movie!"
—James Stewart

In my movie *Querelle,* Brad Davis plays a sailor. He wears pants so tight that you know what religion he isn't.

—Rainer Werner Fassbinder

☆ ☆ ☆ ☆

Elizabeth Taylor is still a primitive—sort of the Grandma Moses of acting.

—Joseph L. Mankiewicz

☆ ☆ ☆ ☆

Gable had only one rule. He always quit at five—I think so he could start drinking. Gable was quite a drinker....In the evening he was a very heavy drinker. As a matter of fact, he told me once that if he couldn't drink he'd just as soon die.

—Edward Dmytryk

☆ ☆ ☆ ☆

Barbara Stanwyck sent me a letter when I signed to direct *Now, Voyager.* "Dear Irving, You are going to do a picture with Bette Davis. Don't you know there are such things as fresh air and sunshine?"

—Irving Rapper

☆ ☆ ☆ ☆

Ruth Gordon worried that *Harold and Maude* might not be believable, because the boy is in love with her, and she's about eighty and they have an affair. She didn't know if she was up to such an illusion. Until I gave her a little tip. I told her to pretend she was an older *man.* "*Now* I can believe it," she said.

—Hal Ashby

☆ ☆ ☆ ☆

Joan Crawford was not that self-confident, despite her image. On the set, she employed a man who paid her compliments. Right before a scene, she would have him whisper things in her ear like "Miss Crawford, you are a great actress" or "Miss Crawford, you are beautiful and ageless." It was like paid hypnosis, and it worked.

—Edmund Goulding

Always I have been ahead of my times. I defied the censors. I was the first to intimate fellatio, in my film *Hurry Sundown*. I had Jane Fonda playing a big, sexy saxophone. She played it between Michael Caine's legs....The critics, they tell me, were merciless. But critics are jealous; like eunuchs, they can watch, but cannot perform.

—Otto Preminger

☆ ☆ ☆ ☆

Among other things, I directed Tarzan movies. Give me an actor like Johnny Weissmuller anytime. This was before all this Method crap and actors scratching their groins for "motivation." If I saw Weissmuller scratching his groin, I knew either his loincloth was too tight or he was pulling at his foreskin. A very uncomplicated actor.

—Richard Thorpe

☆ ☆ ☆ ☆

One of the most unpleasant working experiences I've had was with an actress called Anouk Aimée. [*Justine*] could have been much more than it was...[but her] attitude...intractable. Like Marilyn, but without the results. Let me tell you, that girl knew she'd probably never work in Hollywood again, or she'd never have defied me like that....She *belongs* in European movies.

—George Cukor

☆ ☆ ☆ ☆

I've finished directing Jane Fonda and Robert De Niro in *Stanley and Iris*. Reporters ask me what it was like, working with these two big stars. Was there temperament? I tell them, "You want temperament, ask me about my last movie, *Nuts*." It starred Barbra Streisand, who also produced it. They ask me, "Was she tough to work with?" I tell them, "Don't ask me. Ask my predecessor—the director she fired...."

—Martin Ritt

☆ ☆ ☆ ☆

You work with a young star, a budding star, a potential star, and just because you're a director you're supposed to know who has star quality, who's going to be the next big tornado. It's not always easy to spot star quality, to recognize a star—a lot depends on whether the studio agrees with you and agrees to give someone the star buildup....It's easier to recognize who doesn't have star quality, who's going to be a working actor or a secondary actor.

In *Rebel Without a Cause*, I saw that Natalie [Wood] had strong possibilities; limited talent, but a star buildup would take her far. Sal Mineo had star possibilities, too, but only into his twenties, say. Dennis Hopper, he'd already worked for me before, but his eyes are too empty, his lips are too tight. If he stays in the business, he'll keep working, but he won't be a star.

With Jimmy [Dean], the star quality's there, hitting you in the face. But it was obvious, too soon, that self-discipline and self-nurturing were out of his reach. Star quality in and of itself is not a guarantee, is not necessarily a positive thing.

—Nicholas Ray

☆ ☆ ☆ ☆

There, darling, that's what I wanted. I knew you could do it.
—D. W. Griffith after slapping Mabel Normand [in 1912] so she could do a crying scene in *The Mender of Nets*

☆ ☆ ☆ ☆

Jane Fonda wants to be loved. Lily Tomlin wants to be lovely. Dolly Parton wants to be lovable. In short, Jane and Lily want what they don't have, while Dolly only wants to take her lovability into a new medium....It's her [Dolly's] first movie, so unlike Jane and Lily, she's playing a character very much like herself. Damn near identical, in fact.

—Colin Higgins, *Nine to Five*

☆ ☆ ☆ ☆

[*Boom*] was miscast. Regardless how big your stars, miscasting means a missed opportunity to tell the story properly. Tennessee Williams's play was about a rich older woman using and being used by a much younger gigolo. It had Tallulah Bankhead and Tab Hunter. It had homoerotic undertones, and it flopped. We had Elizabeth Taylor and Richard, who were too close in age for their characters and who were a husband-and-wife act. *It* flopped. Who the hell knows anything?

—Joseph Losey

She has lilacs for pubic hairs.
—Blake Edwards on Julie Andrews

✰ ✰ ✰

The press and the public want to believe that what they see on the screen is the truth. After *The World of Suzie Wong* became a hit around the world, everyone would corner me at parties and beg me to reveal whether Bill Holden and Nancy Kwan had really had an affair. The tone of the voices and the look in the eyes made clear that they fervently hoped there had been an affair. I almost felt guilty disappointing them, telling them that Bill's sons were about Nancy's age and that off the set she spent more time playing tennis with them, while Bill was tending to his local real estate interests.
—Richard Quine

✰ ✰ ✰

People see her in my film [*Greed*] and exclaim it was the only serious, worthwhile thing she ever did. She later goes into comedy, to exaggerate her eyes and hands [movements], and never again they allow her to play dramatic. She ruins her serious career by being too much herself!
—Erich Von Stroheim on Zasu Pitts

✰ ✰ ✰

Dirk Bogarde is a fine actor. His problem is breaking through his own coldness and emotional hostility to his softer, guarded emotions. I may reasonably say that he is the least friendly or outgoing actor I've ever worked with.
—Joseph Losey

✰ ✰ ✰

If I work in Hollywood, it might be not so good. They might tell each other I am pushy, like Streisand.
—Lina Wertmuller, the Italian director who is the only woman ever nominated for an Academy Award for Best Director

✰ ✰ ✰

I've heard his nickname—Rotten Cotten. When I've worked with Joe, I've found him cooperative and giving of his best. He's not a tour de force actor; even Orson Welles didn't work miracles with him. I'd work with Joe again. However, it is true that post-Welles, he treats moviemaking less as a craft and more as a well-dressed social occasion.

—Robert Aldrich

☆ ☆ ☆ ☆

Kim Novak has been seriously hurt by men. Unlike Marilyn, she survived. But her pain has also survived, and she no longer trusts men, particularly if they want to become or seem to be getting intimate. So I have to be careful to remain fatherly and detached when guiding her through her roles. In *The Legend of Lylah Clare* she plays two roles, two actresses, one of them a late star, a legend in the Dietrich-Garbo persona who is sapphic. I have no trouble ignoring Kim's beauty, because I just think of her as being sapphic, like Lylah....

—Robert Aldrich

☆ ☆ ☆ ☆

[In *The Hotel New Hampshire*] Nastassja Kinski and Jodie Foster have an affair. I did it very well. I kept my emotional distance. I wasn't at all jealous.

—Tony Richardson

☆ ☆ ☆ ☆

Brando and I, we want to kill each other [during the shooting of *Burn!*], so we decide it is better not to talk to each other, to avoid blood and more unpleasantness.

—Gillo Pontecorvo

☆ ☆ ☆ ☆

I wasn't at *all* surprised....Of course, I wouldn't be surprised with half the actors I have known!
    —Otto Preminger about learning of Rachel Roberts's suicide

Sean [Connery] is possibly the luckiest actor working, especially at that level of remuneration. He had one popular characterization [James Bond], and on the strength of that, he's gone from film to film and megasalary to megasalary, and quite factually, only his 007s performed that well at the box office.

—Ronald Neame

☆ ☆ ☆ ☆

John Wayne is a son of a bitch, but he's the sort of son of a bitch I like. Montgomery Clift's also a son of a bitch, but I don't like him.

—Howard Hawks

☆ ☆ ☆ ☆

I like Alec Guinness as a man and love him as a talent. But this was long after Charlie Chan and Mr. Moto, and I kept looking at him as a Japanese, and I had to suppress a titter. *A Majority of One* is a good movie. But it's one thing for Roz Russell to make with the Yiddish accent, which she did very well. It's another for Guinness to go sound Japanese—he still doesn't *look* Japanese, and it's not like there's a shortage of Oriental actors or people in the world. Except in Hollywood....Anna May Wong died about the time *A Majority of One* was released. With respect, but maybe the sight of Alec Guinness killed her!

—Mervyn LeRoy

☆ ☆ ☆ ☆

Don't ask me when is [Clint] Eastwood going to do a comedy. Maybe he has done a comedy. If you see his movies and you are not his fan, then maybe is a comedy.

—Sergio Leone

☆ ☆ ☆ ☆

It is good working with Nastassja Kinski on *Tess*. She is young and new, and younger actresses are more pliable than older ones.

—Roman Polanski

Directorial squint: Eastwood

☆ ☆ ☆ ☆

I shouldn't say it, so I will. Kris Kristofferson and Ali MacGraw are crummy actors. But that doesn't mean it [*Convoy*] is a crummy movie, and screw the critics!

—Sam Peckinpah

☆ ☆ ☆ ☆

I had the pleasure of directing Randolph Scott's last movie, a western, of course [*Ride the High Country*]. Randy Scott was a gentleman, and nothing like most western actors. No siree, nothing Neanderthal about Randy Scott.

—Sam Peckinpah

Now I can do to actors what directors did to me—ha-ha! No, I'm just kidding...though I wish Mr. Hitchcock was here, doing his customary cameo bit....

—Anthony Perkins, *Psycho III*

☆ ☆ ☆ ☆

The king of box office is a boy forever.

—Angie Dickinson on Steven Spielberg

☆ ☆ ☆ ☆

[Ron Howard] directed me in some TV movie. He was good. Don't let his TV shows [*The Andy Griffith Show* and *Happy Days*] fool you. And he was respectful, which is almost as important as being good.

—Bette Davis

☆ ☆ ☆ ☆

Wolfgang Petersen directed a very sexy gay love story called *The Consequence*. And last year, *Das Boot* [1981]. And like me, he is an openly gay German. So I don't believe he will ever work in Hollywood, any more than I would. Money is the only reason to work in Hollywood.

—Rainer Werner Fassbinder on the director of the 1993 Clint Eastwood hit *In the Line of Fire*

☆ ☆ ☆ ☆

Raoul Walsh said he informed his actors that he may have only one eye, but he's twice as mean. I got two eyes, and I'm even meaner than Walsh!

—John Huston

☆ ☆ ☆ ☆

I directed Mae West in a big censorship fiasco called *Klondike Annie*. She didn't play a dyke, she played a missionary, and the moralists hated that. Hell, Mae West was the missionary of sex!...I liked Miss West and her pictures, didn't much care for directing her. See, directing her in her scenes wasn't that much more challenging than sitting and watching one of her pictures.

—Raoul Walsh

☆ ☆ ☆ ☆

Mae West was, next to Marie Dressler, the oldest leading lady then working in the movies. Unlike Marie, she wasn't an out-and-out comic; she was supposed to be a very sexy actress who drew humor out of sexual innuendo. It was well known that she took less direction than most actresses, and most of us resented it in those days. Looking back, it makes some sense that an actress in her forties, someone as experienced and successful as Mae West, might know what worked well for her and what didn't.

—Henry Hathaway

☆ ☆ ☆ ☆

At one time, David Lean favored Marlon Brando [to star as *Lawrence of Arabia*]. I was against it. I didn't want the headaches, I didn't want *Marlon of Brando*. This was a production so big, we didn't even require a star....Whoever we cast as Lawrence, I knew he would become a star thanks to the production. Nor did I very much care if I never worked again with Peter O'Toole, whose first picture this is. [It wasn't.] Because when you create a star, you create a monster.

—producer Sam Spiegel

☆ ☆ ☆ ☆

Now foreign directors, it is very popular in America. But not always. In 1950s I have friend make inquiries if Marilyn Monroe is interested to be in one of my movies, for the future. She say no, thank you. Is big star, I am Italian director....She would be divine in the scenes played by Anita Ekberg. But with Marilyn Monroe, whole movie [*La Dolce Vita*] then has to be about the girl in the fountain.

—Federico Fellini

☆ ☆ ☆ ☆

I don't like actors who act. I like actors who are....Alfred Hitchcock was right about actors. But he didn't say they're cattle.

It was a famous misquote. He said actors should be treated like cattle....When you treat them like actors, they freak out. When you treat them like stars, they want to turn on you and kill you.

—Andy Warhol

☆ ☆ ☆ ☆

I'm letting Paul Morrissey codirect some of my stuff....The boring thing about directing is that you have to deal with people instead of things.

—Andy Warhol

☆ ☆ ☆ ☆

Rock Hudson is in my films because he is a handsome cipher. If an actor has too much personality, he projects what he wants to project. With too much uniqueness, he is always himself, never Everyman. With Rock Hudson, female audiences can project their feelings and desires onto him, and the male audiences can assign to him their own hopes and fears. Most Hollywood stars are symbols, not individuals. This keeps actors from getting in the way of the story, for movies are just illustrated, breathing stories.

—Douglas Sirk

☆ ☆ ☆ ☆

I'll say I'm lucky! My first movie, and it's a big-budget musical [*Can't Stop the Music*]! It's got everything...the Village People, hit songs, male nudity, Valerie Perrine and her cleavage, Bruce Jenner and his legs....My producer [Allan Carr] thinks it will be another *Grease*! [It may have been, but it bombed.]

—Nancy Walker

☆ ☆ ☆ ☆

When you direct, you're learning. When you're a teacher, you impart learning. This helps me feel more serene. Directing, I always had people at my back. In the classroom, I have people in front of me—bright, eager pupils....The press can't trivialize teaching. With motion pictures, they tried to reduce your accomplishments to what star you worked with....I didn't want to be known just for making Clara Bow a star.

—Dorothy Arzner

Leave it to Hollywood to take the few genuine no-talents in England, bring them over here, and try and make stars of guys like Stewart Granger and Roger Moore!

—Richard Brooks

☆ ☆ ☆ ☆

In the States, they all think I'm a lady director. They don't use Carol or Beverley or Evelyn there [as first names]. When I became *Sir* Carol, I thought my problems were at an end. However, Trevor [Howard] told me not to expect Americans to use "Sir" very often. "Most of them are too democratic for that," he said.

—Carol Reed

☆ ☆ ☆ ☆

Horses make some of the best actors. I'll take Trigger any day! They don't answer back—especially when they're stuffed.

—Sam Peckinpah

Directors' Cuts—and Vice Versa

John Huston couldn't care less about actresses. Men and horses, that is all! He gives better roles to the horses in his films than to the actresses.

—Delphine Seyrig

☆ ☆ ☆ ☆

Vincente Minnelli was a repressed homosexual who became a bully. So I admit he was successful, because most directors want to be bullies when they grow up.

—Anthony Perkins

☆ ☆ ☆ ☆

We called him son-of-Lubitsch behind his back.

—Mae West on Ernst Lubitsch

☆ ☆ ☆ ☆

Cecil B. DeMille was De phony and De hypocrite of all time. He liked being the biggest fly on the Hollywood shit-hill.

—Yul Brynner

C.B. had a foot fetish. I know. I drove him mad with my feet and actually used my bare feet to get better roles out of him. He definitely did not like actresses with feet of clay!

—Paulette Goddard

☆ ☆ ☆ ☆

Cecil B. DeMille handed me the script of *Northwest Mounted Police,* and when I'd read it he asked how I liked it. I said, "It's the same part I played for you last year. I'll change costumes and play it again," and he said, "You ungrateful son of a bitch, if it wasn't for me, you'd still be parking cars at Santa Anita." He was no director. He didn't know what to tell us. Also, he was not a nice person, politically or any other way. I think the only man DeMille ever envied was Hitler.

—Robert Preston

☆ ☆ ☆ ☆

Ernst Lubitsch was a great director, but he left one no leeway at all, telling you when to light a cigarette, when to put your hands in your pockets, regulating every movement and gesture, every expression. I felt like a robot after a few days.

—Fredric March

☆ ☆ ☆ ☆

John Huston treats me like an idiot—"Honey, this" and "Honey, that."

—Marilyn Monroe

☆ ☆ ☆ ☆

Edmund Goulding did something that drove actors crazy. He'd get out there and act out everybody's roles for them—even the women. And we were supposed to imitate him. We wanted to give our own interpretations.

—Joan Blondell

☆ ☆ ☆ ☆

On *Little Women,* when director George Cukor was ready for us—Kate Hepburn, Jean Parker, Frances Dee, and myself—he'd always say, with a great sense of humor, "Come on, you four little bitches, the set is ready!"

—Joan Bennett

Michael Curtiz was a savage, a real beast. A Hungarian Otto Preminger. He was a tyrant, he was abusive, he was cruel. Oh, he was just a villain, but I guess he was pretty good. We didn't believe it then....

—Olivia de Havilland

☆ ☆ ☆ ☆

Billy Wilder-than-what? He's a fine writer, but as a director, I found him weak as water.

—Klaus Kinski

☆ ☆ ☆ ☆

That dreadful picture [*The Producers*]. I can't bear to watch it, even on a small television. I'm rather sorry I did it. I must have needed the money—living in Hollywood weakens one's motives. [Mel Brooks] reminds me of the saying that nobody ever went broke underestimating the American public's taste....His first films were his best. But that is not saying much....*That* picture, I believe, was his first.

—Estelle Winwood

☆ ☆ ☆ ☆

I was directed by the great Dorothy Arzner. She was a lesbian, but not really aggressive. Only when some big bully opposed her hard-won authority. With us actors, she was docile and very quiet. One of the actors had a nickname for her—Little Miss Mouse Fart.

—Merle Oberon

☆ ☆ ☆ ☆

I was in Hitchcock's *Lifeboat*. So was Tallulah Bankhead, who didn't wear panties, and each morning when we climbed into a lifeboat—up on a mechanical rocker—she gave the cast and crew a hell of a view, hiking up her skirt! Eventually someone complained to Hitch, who didn't want to get involved. He explained that it was an interdepartmental matter—involving wardrobe, costume, and possibly hairdressing....

—Hume Cronyn

William Wyler would ruin a lot of takes on *Funny Girl*. He'd smoke and cough. The smoke would get in front of the lens....
—Barbra Streisand

☆ ☆ ☆ ☆

John Ford was so egomaniacal. He would never rehearse, didn't want to talk about a part. If an actor started to ask questions, he'd either take those pages and tear them out of the script or insult him in an awful way. He loved getting his shot in the first take, which for him meant it was fresh. He would print the first take even if it wasn't any good.
—Henry Fonda

☆ ☆ ☆ ☆

Joshua Logan was directing Brando in *Sayonara*, and he had a crush on him, but he also feared and resented him, and he totally despised me, because I got to know Marlon very well, and I got that famous, notorious interview with Marlon. Josh—who was manic-depressive and crazy as a bedbug—never knew for sure what else I might have gotten out of Brando....
—Truman Capote

☆ ☆ ☆ ☆

They can ruin your book in two ways....They cast Audrey Hepburn in my *Breakfast at Tiffany's*, and I adore Audrey, but she was miscast—she is no hillbilly! Nor, really, a tomboy. Jodie Foster would be ideal, in a remake....But worst of all, they chose a horrible director, Blake Edwards, who I could spit on! *And* they cast Mickey Rooney as a Japanese—I just wanted to throw up!
—Truman Capote

☆ ☆ ☆ ☆

Roberto [Rossellini] was so domineering, very Italian. Actresses hated him, but I knew he was brilliant...with time, I liked it less and less, and when he would bark an order at me, sometimes I would forget we were married and shout back, "Who do you think you are, my husband?" Naturally, with time, we had to cease both associations; the magic was gone.
—Ingrid Bergman

Otto Preminger is a great showman, but very weird. No understanding of actors. I swear, he would creep up behind a nervous actor on a tense set and scream at them, *"Relax!"* And then he was angry and disappointed when, for some reason, that didn't relax you.

—Sal Mineo

☆ ☆ ☆ ☆

Otto Preminger is a sadist, pure and simple....He chose me to star in *The Cardinal,* and then he was cruel and evil and homophobic. He robbed me of the joy of acting and drove me into psychoanalysis. Perhaps I should be grateful: I became a bigger author than I was a star, and as a novelist, *I'm* the director—no bosses!

—Tom Tryon

☆ ☆ ☆ ☆

I read the book *Such Good Friends* and called my agent and said, "I want to do this part." She said, "Otto Preminger is directing it." I was warned about him, but could anybody really be *that* bad?...I have been the victim of some killers in my time. He's one of the biggest. He's a *horrible* man. I was absolutely destroyed by that man. *Phew!* But who ever hears of him anymore? Is he still alive?

—Dyan Cannon

☆ ☆ ☆ ☆

I thank God that neither I nor any member of my family will ever be so hard up that we have to work for Otto Preminger!

—Lana Turner

☆ ☆ ☆ ☆

Woody Allen has this mensch image, but he's smug and superior, especially with women. In *Hannah and Her Sisters,* he was openly abusive of Mia [Farrow]. He'd call names, very manipulative, and no respect for age, either—he was rude to Mia's mother, Maureen [O'Sullivan], who played opposite me....He's a very cold man, probably very troubled.

—Lloyd Nolan

Steven Spielberg always wanted to be a little boy when he grew up.

—Rainer Werner Fassbinder

☆ ☆ ☆ ☆

I worked with Marlon Brando on the stage in *Truckline Cafe* and then on the screen. Then he directed me in *One-Eyed Jacks*, at that time famous for its cost and length. It was Marlon's first and last directorial effort. If *Jacks* had been a success, he might by now have directed another. I think all that criticism got to him. He may be too thin-skinned to keep directing....

—Karl Malden

☆ ☆ ☆ ☆

I'm no shrimp, and I've noticed that directors are usually frustrated actors. They're lethally vain. If a director is shorter and heavier than his male lead, he usually resents him. I've found this to be the case, no question, from Cukor to Hitchcock to Sidney Lumet....You can't be a chum to most directors, because they envy you too much. Even if they're outwardly polite, there's always an underlying tension. The only director and actor that I can come up with that I heard got along really well recently are Robert Downey Sr. and Robert Downey Jr. (on *Too Much Sun*). Because they're father and son. Even then, they probably wouldn't have got along so great if Junior wasn't shorter than Senior. Trust me, directors are funny that way!

—Anthony Perkins

☆ ☆ ☆ ☆

I like to think that every director I've worked with has fallen a little in love with me. I know Dorothy Arzner did.

—Joan Crawford

☆ ☆ ☆ ☆

It was unusual, to say the least, playing Barbra Streisand's wife in *Yentl*. But as a director, she was very generous, very protective. She treated me something like her own toy doll at times.

—Amy Irving

☆ ☆ ☆ ☆

I worked with Anne Bancroft in the only movie she directed. It was called *Fatso,* and I played the title role. You might say I grew into the role.

—Dom DeLuise

☆ ☆ ☆ ☆

I have nothing but praise for Ida Lupino. She's a pro's pro, and she can be as bossy as any man when she needs to be. And a director often needs to be!

—Rosalind Russell, *The Trouble with Angels*

☆ ☆ ☆ ☆

Dorothy Arzner was rather remarkable, now that I look back. She didn't spend time talking about being a woman and directing; she just went ahead and did it.... She directed me in my first

Mother figure Ida Lupino

starring role [*Christopher Strong*]. She made it look so easy. Greenhorn that I was, I thought I might like to direct someday, myself. Of course the idea of an actress directing a picture—they would have laughed me right off the set. Because it's power, you know, it's budgets. Even twenty years later, I still wouldn't have had a prayer of getting a picture to direct...and I'm afraid I'd have been inclined to be too manipulative and argumentative!

—Katharine Hepburn

☆ ☆ ☆ ☆

...a full-fledged monster.
—columnist Joyce Haber on Barbra Streisand, who reportedly bossed William Wyler, the director of her first film

☆ ☆ ☆ ☆

Menahem Golan should stick to producing. Money, not art, is his favorite subject. Every time he directs, it's the Golan Depths.

—Aldo Ray

☆ ☆ ☆ ☆

Cecil B. DeMille had dementia peacock. When we were making *Samson and Delilah,* he brought in peacock feathers for Hedy Lamarr's famous peacock gown. He had his own peacocks at home, created in his own image. The damned gown got more publicity than any scene in the damned picture, and when we shot the scene with the feathered gown, C.B. paid more attention to whether Hedy Lamarr was molting than to Samson, me, the temple, or anything else!

—George Sanders

☆ ☆ ☆ ☆

I was bamboozled into doing the worst picture of my career [*The Heat's On*] by a smooth-talking Russian fast talker named Gregory Ratoff—accent on the *Rat*!

—Mae West

☆ ☆ ☆ ☆

I was in *Everything You Always Wanted to Know About Sex (But Were Afraid to Ask)*. Woody Allen was the director. When I met him, I wondered how he could possibly be qualified to direct this movie.

—John Carradine

☆ ☆ ☆ ☆

I was in *Portnoy's Complaint*, and my complaint is people in this business who think they can do everything. Ernest Lehman is an A-1 writer. He's written some of the best movies. Why he thought it wasn't enough and chose to helm *Portnoy's Complaint* is a quandary to me....*Portnoy's Complaint* was a funny, entertaining, clever novel. [But] as a movie, it was a jerk-off. The worst jerks in this business, though, are the directors who think they can write. Directors can't do anything but direct—otherwise, they wouldn't be directors! Actors can direct, and writers can direct, but directors are *stuck*.

—John Carradine

☆ ☆ ☆ ☆

I don't think Blake Edwards will ever receive as much respect as he feels he's entitled to.

—William Holden

☆ ☆ ☆ ☆

There are two kinds of intelligent people in this world. The one who uses his intelligence for the good, who's willing to share it. And the one who uses it like a weapon or to keep people from getting too close. The second kind is Billy Wilder.

—William Holden

☆ ☆ ☆ ☆

I did an audition for Tony Richardson in the late 1970s. For a medium-sized film role; the way he was presenting it, you'd have thought it was the starring part. I eventually asked him, "Are you nervous about my being in your film? Singers can act, you know." He answered, "I know. But can you pass for straight?" I was flabbergasted, but without pausing, I answered back, "Can you?"

He smiled like the Cheshire cat and said, "I do." End of session, and I didn't get the part. Later, I tell a friend who's done Broadway and the West End, "I had no idea Tony Richardson is gay." He answered, "He's not. He's bi." Well, excuse me! I'm bicoastal, myself....Now he's died of AIDS. What a tragic pretense.

> —openly gay Peter Allen, who died of AIDS
> the following year, in 1992

☆ ☆ ☆ ☆

[Jean-Luc] Godard is the only person I've ever met who's truly revolutionary. But a true revolutionary has to care about people. Godard doesn't really care enough.

> —Jane Fonda

☆ ☆ ☆ ☆

John Schlesinger is an artist of the first rank. But he makes me glad I'm Welsh. He is so veiled, so distant, always camouflaging his boredom or mistrust with good manners and tiny smiles. He made me want to scream at him, "Get *real*, John! Let your hair down!" On second thought, one wouldn't want to say *that* to a bald director!

> —Rachel Roberts

☆ ☆ ☆ ☆

John Huston is a helmsman and a ham. Far too much of a ham to ever give up acting and hide his ego behind a camera.

> —George Sanders

☆ ☆ ☆ ☆

He was in love with both of us [her and Richard Gere] at the same time. To be kind, you can say he was taking our characteristics from his own nature, from his male and female sides.
> —Lauren Hutton on writer-director Paul Schrader, *American Gigolo*

☆ ☆ ☆ ☆

He's new, but he knows more than he lets on...a refreshing change from the usual—directors who know less than they pretend.

—Joan Crawford on Steven Spielberg

☆ ☆ ☆ ☆

Noel [Coward] did do some directing and codirecting. It's just not a polite enough profession to suit him, though.

—Trevor Howard

☆ ☆ ☆ ☆

Hitchcock didn't concern himself with the performers. He put us through our paces. He preplanned everything...and was more concerned with and even interested in story and sequence. He cast for a type. If someone was a sophisticated blonde, she would do the role justice so far as he was concerned. If you looked like his conception of Mrs. Danvers, then by Hitchcock you'd done a magnificent job of acting the part—even before I'd set foot on the set!

—Judith Anderson

☆ ☆ ☆ ☆

I won the Oscar for *The Razor's Edge*....Edmund Goulding was very theatrical; he wanted badly to act. But he didn't dare risk it. I think he feared losing his dignity. He really wanted to be Clifton Webb, who also had a memorable role in the picture. Clifton was something of a pompous ass, but he had more dignity than any other actor I knew.

—Anne Baxter

☆ ☆ ☆ ☆

John Schlesinger, in my opinion, would love to be a performer. He's thrilled by actors and what we do....Numerous directors would have become actors if they'd had the looks or facilities.

—Peter Finch

☆ ☆ ☆ ☆

A director who used to be a writer isn't much use [to an actor] very often. A writer-director is worse, with this *auteur* nonsense they've imported from France. Filmmaking is a collaboration; it is not comparable to one artist painting a painting by himself....It's better to work with someone like Sydney Pollack, who was an actor before he began directing. He can relate to what actors have to go through. Plus, he had the sense to make a smart career change! If I were a lousy star, I'd certainly try and find something else....

—Natalie Wood

☆ ☆ ☆ ☆

[Alexander] Korda kept offering me small roles in movies that he was offering to Charles [Laughton], in hopes that I would persuade Charles to say yes to him. Considering the size of what he offered Charles, what I was offered was rather insulting, and Charles and I seldom said yes to Mr. Korda!

—Elsa Lanchester

☆ ☆ ☆ ☆

Ken Russell is like a madman painting pictures and making movies in an asylum. He is not boring!

—Rudolf Nureyev

☆ ☆ ☆ ☆

John Waters makes every movie seem more like a party than a business venture, which is what movies are, but keep it under your hat!

—Divine

☆ ☆ ☆ ☆

After we were all done with the interminable *Cleopatra,* Richard Burton made it known to [writer-director] Joseph L. Mankiewicz that regardless whether *Cleopatra* was a success or a failure, he was convinced that it would double the number of his fans. To which Mank replied, "Yes, I heard you married your leading lady."

—Rex Harrison

☆ ☆ ☆ ☆

George Cukor and I are friends. We've never worked together....

—Mae West

I'm proud to have been in a few of the films of Signor Luchino Visconti and proud to call him friend.

—Burt Lancaster

☆ ☆ ☆ ☆

Doing *Querelle* brought us very close together....I cried for two weeks after I heard he'd died.

—Brad Davis on Rainer Werner Fassbinder

☆ ☆ ☆ ☆

I discovered Jack Lemmon, a fine actor....He's not one of those actors who'll bore you to death discussing acting. He'd rather bore you to death discussing golf.

—director George Cukor

☆ ☆ ☆ ☆

My mom told me that Robert Altman told her I have no personality. I have one, I must have one, but I don't quite know what it is.

—Jennifer Jason Leigh

☆ ☆ ☆ ☆

Clint Eastwood has two expressions on camera: sullen and angry. Off camera, he has one: very, very rich.

—director Don Siegel

☆ ☆ ☆ ☆

I don't like to generalize, for I've directed several actors who earned Academy Awards for our—sorry, their—performances. But in general, actresses are easier to work with in one respect. They offer me less resistance. Except Katharine Hepburn, who resists everyone, on principle. But most actresses place themselves entirely in my hands. If I were so inclined (heterosexual), I could get away with murder!

—George Cukor

☆ ☆ ☆ ☆

Sometimes a director is jealous of you. This occurred most recently with Franco Zeffirelli, who is flamboyant even by

Italian standards. It wasn't an easy collaboration....I am more comfortable with a director who is obsessed with his project instead of one who wishes to be me. Some would wish to *have* me, except now I'm too old for them!

—Laurence Olivier

☆ ☆ ☆ ☆

"Rich and Famous:" Candice Bergen, George Cukor, and Jacqueline Bisset

"Endless Love:" Brooke Shields, Franco Zeffirelli, and Martin Hewitt

I once heard that Garbo had been approached by one of her directors, a married man. She was furious! She told her friends, "Is he so stupid to believe I am a loose woman, like the womans they make me play?" You see, some of us developed crushes on our directors, or went even further. But I have it on good authority that Garbo was happiest when she could think of her director as a brother. Oh, brother!

—Bette Davis

☆ ☆ ☆ ☆

I'd rather leave directing to the directors. I'd find it distracting to be directed by a Paul Newman. Costarring with him is fine. But I like my directors to be father figures. If Paul directed me, I'd be committing mental incest.

—Ava Gardner

Paul Newman, a distracting director

☆ ☆ ☆ ☆

Let's Get Physical!

☆ ☆ ☆ ☆

That broad's got a great future behind her....
> —Constance Bennett on newcomer Marilyn Monroe

☆ ☆ ☆

Marilyn Monroe was a glorified transvestite.

> —Boy George

☆ ☆ ☆

Marilyn got agoraphobia, which was just one of her problems. She'd go to the hairdresser in the morning, then go home and stay there all day. She had a beautiful complexion, but when the camera would start rolling, she'd break out in a rash. I had a theory that if the camera began to roll, she'd start to menstruate—she was that vulnerable.

> —Robert Mitchum

☆ ☆ ☆

Every other actress in Hollywood has had a nose job, from the Gabors to Marlo Thomas and Marilyn Monroe. Marilyn was sensitive about hers, even though she only had the tip done. A

242

nose job was just part of her ordeal in climbing to the top. When she was tipsy, she might break down and tell you how she'd also had to offer blow jobs to climb that ladder of success—wrong by wrong.

—Peter Lawford

☆ ☆ ☆ ☆

In the 1950s she [Audrey Hepburn] had a great influence on how women in Europe and America wanted to look. It was more realistic for them to become like her than like Marilyn Monroe!

—Luchino Visconti

☆ ☆ ☆ ☆

Audrey Hepburn is the patron saint of the anorexics.

—Orson Welles

☆ ☆ ☆ ☆

[Maria] Callas admired Miss Hepburn in *Roman Holiday*, and from then on she taped her photographs to her walls, in the kitchen, everywhere. She almost starved herself. Of course, *then* she could play almost anything she chose....

—Luchino Visconti

☆ ☆ ☆ ☆

Paul [Newman] is a little paunchy, even though he doesn't eat desserts. Popcorn's his dessert—one of them....

—Rock Hudson

☆ ☆ ☆ ☆

All my life I wanted to look like Elizabeth Taylor. Now I find that Liz Taylor is beginning to look like me.

—Divine, who weighed three hundred pounds.

☆ ☆ ☆ ☆

Dietrich? She's okay, if you like cheekbones, dahling.

—Tallulah Bankhead

Tony Curtis is a perfect example of what ambition and bad career choices can do to fabulous good looks over the years....
—John Gielgud

☆ ☆ ☆ ☆

There are two good reasons why men will go to see her.
—Howard Hughes on Jane Russell

☆ ☆ ☆ ☆

I pity any actor who gets second billing to Raquel Welch. He's really getting third billing to her breasts!
—Edward G. Robinson

☆ ☆ ☆ ☆

Raquel Welch is silicone from the neck down. Or so I have heard. But she will only admit to a nose job. She says she corrected what she calls her "Latin nose." What the hell is a Latin nose? I am myself a Latin, and my nose is most decorative!
—Fernando Lamas

☆ ☆ ☆ ☆

I was on television, and somebody asked me what did I think of Jacqueline Susann. I said, "She looks like a truck driver in drag." She was watching the show, and she fell out of bed....She sued me for a million dollars, but she was told that she had better drop that lawsuit because all they had to do is bring ten truck drivers into court and put them on the witness stand and you've lost your case. Because she *did* look like a truck driver in drag.
—Truman Capote

☆ ☆ ☆ ☆

I was invited to a screening of *Samson and Delilah,* starring Victor Mature and Hedy Lamarr. Afterward, one of the studio brass asked me how I liked it. I replied, "I never like a movie where the hero's tits are bigger than the heroine's.
—Groucho Marx

Fred Astaire was almost as concerned with his toupee looking right as he was with perfecting each dance number.

—choreographer Hermes Pan

☆ ☆ ☆ ☆

I've never known a vainer man....He constantly complained about his legs, which he considered too short.

—Marlene Dietrich on Rudolf Nureyev

☆ ☆ ☆ ☆

I always felt sorry for Herbert Marshall because of his wooden leg. Of course, we never mentioned it. One day, he and I were chatting, and I saw the columnist Sheilah Graham heading our way. I told him without thinking, "Oh, Bart, watch out for her. She'll talk your leg off."

—Joan Fontaine

☆ ☆ ☆ ☆

Today's actors are more handsome; the actresses are not....Then Herbert Marshall was a star, even a romantic symbol, although he had lost a leg in the First [World] War. There was a famous story that he was once the houseguest of a famous hostess, and he tripped in her house and seemed to be in pain. So she rushed to her husband and asked him whether she should call a doctor or a carpenter?

—Marlene Dietrich

☆ ☆ ☆ ☆

He's an idiot, like a big cheesecake on legs.

—Boy George on Andy Warhol

☆ ☆ ☆ ☆

He looks like a dwarf that fell into a vat of pubic hair.

—Boy George on Prince

Sleeping with George Michael would be like having sex with a groundhog.

—Boy George

☆ ☆ ☆ ☆

They say the two best-hung men in Hollywood are Forrest Tucker and Milton Berle. What a shame—it's never the handsome ones. The bigger they are, the homelier.

—Betty Grable

☆ ☆ ☆ ☆

Doing love scenes with Clarke Gable in *Gone With the Wind* was not that romantic. His dentures smelled something awful.

—Vivien Leigh

☆ ☆ ☆ ☆

To keep my mouth fresh for those [kissing] clinches I chewed gum, and during takes I would poke a wad up next to my teeth. But once, Clark kissed me too forcefully. When he drew back, we were attached by a ribbon of sticky gum! I shrieked with laughter as Clark glumly picked the gum from his [false] teeth. From then on, I gargled.

—Lana Turner

☆ ☆ ☆ ☆

One day [producer] Hal Wallis approached me with a $5,000 bonus if I could make Joseph Cotten have an erection during a scene. Wallis said, "Joe is such a gentleman. He's made no approach to his leading ladies...." During our love scene, I leaned against him, but I could not feel any swelling of his organ....My tongue intensely searched Joe's mouth. I could see him react with shock. When I separated from our embrace, suddenly teeth flew out of his mouth in my direction. In my ardor I had dislodged his partial bridge!

—Corinne Calvet

☆ ☆ ☆ ☆

I never worked with him, but I had a brief crush on Gable. One day, I happened to mention it to my dentist, in his office. I was fairly new to Los Angeles, but a few dentists serviced most of the stars. This one was also Gable's dentist, and he asked what I particularly liked about Gable. I said, "His bright smile." He said, "Would you like to see that bright smile today?"

My heart was pounding. I thought Gable must be the next patient, after me. I could hardly wait for the session to end, and then the dentist led me to an adjoining room, and there, under glass, was a pair of Gable's very white dentures....

—Bette Davis

☆ ☆ ☆ ☆

The best ears of our lives.

—Milton Berle on Gable

☆ ☆ ☆ ☆

Bing Crosby had the sticking-out ears of a pixie and the aloof demeanor of a camel.

—Ingrid Bergman

☆ ☆ ☆ ☆

I did a movie with Duke Wayne and was very surprised to find out he had small feet, wore lifts and a corset. Hollywood is seldom what it seems....

—Rock Hudson

☆ ☆ ☆ ☆

The bland leading-lady blonde.

—Robert Morley on Kim Basinger

☆ ☆ ☆ ☆

Most comics are not handsome. Steve [Martin] is. As long as he keeps his mouth shut. When he talks, he kills the hunk image. Oddly enough, in private Steve is shy and reserved. While in public he never shuts up.

—Rachel Ward

☆ ☆ ☆ ☆

Most short men are sort of insecure. Look at Dick Cavett. But Nick Adams had a lifelong love affair with himself. Of course, that's not difficult when you're gay.

—Truman Capote

☆ ☆ ☆ ☆

Tom Arnold was a third-rate comedian. Then he married Roseanne. Great example of a guy who made something of himself, by the sweat of his frau. Or is it the sweat of his sow?

—Pinky Lee

☆ ☆ ☆ ☆

Where else but in America can a poor black boy like Michael Jackson grow up to be a rich white woman?

—Red Buttons

☆ ☆ ☆ ☆

John Wayne had four-inch lifts in his shoes. He had the overheads on his boat accommodated to fit him. He had a special roof put in his station wagon.... The son of a bitch, they probably buried him in his goddamn lifts.

—Robert Mitchum

☆ ☆ ☆ ☆

A very nice man, and genial. Perhaps because he was fat. I like fat people. A wonderful director, of course, as everyone knows.
—Luchino Visconti on George Cukor

☆ ☆ ☆ ☆

Isadora [Duncan] was by no means a lithe or lovely woman! She was plump and "handsome." Yet when people think of her now, they see Vanessa Redgrave [who portrayed her on the screen].
—Elsa Lanchester

☆ ☆ ☆ ☆

Robert Morley is a legend in his own lunchtime.

—Rex Harrison

[Hermione Gingold]: The last time I saw her, she snubbed me. Cut me dead. I said so to a friend of mine. My friend said it must have been because *I* stayed thin....

—Estelle Winwood

☆ ☆ ☆ ☆

Liz Taylor should be grateful to me—my jokes are one of the reasons she went on a diet. It was embarrassing. When I took her to Sea World and Shamu the Whale jumped out of the water, she asked if it came with vegetables.

—Joan Rivers

☆ ☆ ☆ ☆

Mae West wanted to buy a new convertible car, so she went to the showroom and tried out the latest model. She decided thanks, but no, thanks. The car dealer said, "Why not? It's got every luxury, from a car radio to bucket seats." Mae said, "I know. But your bucket seats aren't big enough for my buckets...."

—Debbie Reynolds

☆ ☆ ☆ ☆

A tabloid printed a fictitious article quoting me saying that I keep in shape but the other old M-G-M stars like Esther Williams were falling apart. Esther wrote me the most vitriolic letter I have ever received from any human being, threatening to pull every hair out of my head and using words no truck driver ever heard of!

—Ann Miller

☆ ☆ ☆ ☆

[Noel Coward] tried to advise me. I recall it precisely. He said, "A polo jumper or unfortunate tie exposes one to danger."

—Cecil Beaton

☆ ☆ ☆ ☆

I *told* Noel when he began to gain all the weight, and he took it personally. It was meant aesthetically; he worshipped beauty, and don't we all.

—Cecil Beaton

Funny about both Margaret Rutherford and Margaret Hamilton [the Wicked Witch in *The Wizard of Oz*]. Both were dreadfully plain in their youth. The older they got, the easier they were to look at....Age brings down great beauties, but it's also an equalizer—it makes ugly young women into nice-looking old ladies. Time does heal some wounds. For some people.

—Estelle Winwood

☆ ☆ ☆ ☆

Hollywood? Don't speak ill of the dead. Who have we got? Elliott Gould, Richard Benjamin, and Dustin Hoffman. If those guys had been my roommates in college, I couldn't have got them a date.

—Mort Sahl

☆ ☆ ☆ ☆

She has a face that belongs to the sea and the wind, with large rocking-horse nostrils and teeth that you just know bite an apple every day.

—Cecil Beaton on Katharine Hepburn

☆ ☆ ☆ ☆

Katharine Hepburn sounds more and more like Donald Duck.

—Liberace

☆ ☆ ☆ ☆

Have you met Jack Palance? He once played Attila the Hun. The man is frightening! If there really were a Dracula, he'd be it.

—Judith Anderson

☆ ☆ ☆ ☆

I'll tell you why Brigitte Bardot never became a Hollywood star. Two reasons: She went naked on screen too often—where's the hidden allure in that? And she has a boyish ass. Most American men do not like boyish asses.

—Sammy Davis Jr.

Claudette Colbert was pretty rather than beautiful; she had some difficult angles to her face.... The right side of her face was called "the other side of the moon," because nobody ever saw it.

—Mary Astor

☆ ☆ ☆ ☆

Two profiles pasted together.

—Dorothy Parker on Basil Rathbone

☆ ☆ ☆ ☆

Only stupid people are confident at an early age.... I was self-conscious about my height—to me, over six feet was a giraffe. I wanted to be shorter, whereas most of today's actors are shorter and want to be taller.... Today I love my height, among other things. But... I couldn't do a biography of Toulouse-Lautrec. I couldn't do *The Dustin Hoffman Story*....

—Rock Hudson

☆ ☆ ☆ ☆

Sly Stallone is five-seven I believe. Shorter than you'd think—not just short on talent. Anyway, he only hires actors his height or shorter, unless they're to play some kind of freakish villain. So I'll never work with Stallone unless I let him shoot me, and I'll never let myself get *that* desperate!

—Burt Lancaster

☆ ☆ ☆ ☆

Lana [Cantrell] wasn't beautiful, but stunningly handsome, and she attracted men without ever trying at all.... Johnny Carson had such a thing for her; she was on the show at first once a month. But despite his best-laid plans, he could never get alone with her. At one point, Lana, Johnny, Doc Severinsen, and I had dinner. Then Lana and I went off together. It was obvious we were together. Johnny never spoke to me after that.

—Judy Carne

☆ ☆ ☆ ☆

[Beatrice Lillie]: I politely suggested that she might experiment with a new hairstyle, something less boyish. She took offense, and said I shouldn't interfere in her private life. The cheek of it! I was merely commenting on her bloody hair.

—Estelle Winwood

☆ ☆ ☆ ☆

Orson Welles always carries with him a little suitcase with his makeup. He never appears in a film with his real nose. He's ashamed of his small nose. He has to stick something on his nose, some putty.

—Jeanne Moreau

☆ ☆ ☆ ☆

I've met them all....Peter Lorre looks like a hard-boiled egg— actually, his eyes look like two hard-boiled eggs. Speaking of good eggs, Robert Taylor isn't. Have you met him? He's not just hard-boiled; he's twenty minutes!

—Donna Reed

☆ ☆ ☆ ☆

Harry Cohn was an A-1 stinker. Nickname: Genghis Cohn. He once interviewed me, with an eye toward hiring me. As you may know, I lost my right eye at three, and he wouldn't come out and say it—he kept referring to my "deficiency." I thought he meant a vitamin deficiency or something. Then he tells me I'm off-center on my vision and it'll show on the screen. So I do a screen test to prove that it doesn't, and he calls me back into his office and explains, "Thank you, Mr. Falk, but for the same money I can get an actor with two eyes."

—Peter Falk

☆ ☆ ☆ ☆

I found out Carole [Lombard] wasn't a natural blonde. We're in her dressing room, talking. She starts undressing. I didn't know what to do....She's talking away and mixing peroxide and some other liquid in a bowl. With a piece of cotton she begins to apply the liquid to dye the hair around her honeypot. She glanced up, and saw my amazed look, and smiled. "Relax, Georgie, I'm just making my collar and cuffs match."

—George Raft

☆ ☆ ☆ ☆

Carole Lombard had a marvelous figure. She was sleek and flat-chested, and that was the Look in the 1920s, when we both started. I was a little self-conscious about my bosom. Believe me, I wasn't exactly delighted when I did a picture called *The Boob!*...In the 1930s, bosoms came back in again, so I was in luck, but Carole required some artificial help. Before she would go before the cameras, she was famous for yelling out to her costumers, "Bring me my breasts!"

—Joan Crawford

☆ ☆ ☆ ☆

I've got everything Betty Grable has—only I've had it longer.

—Dame May Whitty

☆ ☆ ☆ ☆

I have nothing to be embarrassed about, and I'm not the first star to be well equipped, though I daresay I'm more munificent [sic] than most! Someone asked Marie McDonald if she minded being nicknamed the Body, and she said that in Hollywood a girl doesn't get very far being known as the Brain....

—Jayne Mansfield

☆ ☆ ☆ ☆

I can match bottoms with anyone in Hollywood!
  —Mia Farrow, after wedding Frank Sinatra and hearing Ava
      Gardner's quote about her boyish appeal

☆ ☆ ☆ ☆

If David Bowie's latest persona is the Thin White Duke, he's going to give a bad name to whites, thin people, and peers of the realm.

—Freddie Mercury

Ann Sothern is a lovely person, a fine actress. She has been underrated, but she has lost her sense of self-discipline—she no longer believes in eating on an empty stomach!

—Bette Davis

☆ ☆ ☆ ☆

Catherine Deneuve told me that in your forties you have to choose between your face and your derriere.

—Lauren Hutton

☆ ☆ ☆ ☆

I used to think Elvis Presley seemed unwholesome—as did much of the public. But he looks like a choirboy next to this singer they call Prince. I don't agree that Elvis Presley is the king of rock and roll, but if he were, Prince would be the toadstool.

—James Mason

☆ ☆ ☆ ☆

Inger Stevens had true beauty, and she had radiance, two different qualities. Not that beauty is a quality, since you don't earn it. The most you can do with beauty is to not go out in the sun and wrinkle it or eat it away with food....But she killed herself, yet another sad proof that beauty can't buy happiness, even for an actress.

—Yul Brynner

☆ ☆ ☆ ☆

Americans want to divide all women into "pretty" or "ugly." In French, we have a word, *jolie-laide*; it is a combination of the two, and it suits a lot of actresses...like Sandra Bernhard.

—Yves Montand

☆ ☆ ☆ ☆

Remember all that lunacy over "the Farrah look"? Thank God that's past! There was even a whole book on how to create the look! If someone really wanted their hair to look like that, all she had to do was go out and buy a stiff, blond, wiggy-looking wig.

—Sandy Dennis

Didn't Orson Welles look porcine to you? I don't mean his weight, necessarily. His *face*—he had a piggy-looking face...something around the nostrils. I always thought that if they filmed George Orwell's *Animal Farm* with human actors, Orson could play the head pig who took over the farm.

—Lucille Ball

☆ ☆ ☆ ☆

The older she gets, the lighter her hair gets. Which means that her hair is giving her away!

—Gilda Radner on Barbara Walters

☆ ☆ ☆ ☆

Alcohol does things to your face and skin. You don't get away scot-free. Pretense is futile. Look at Tallulah Bankhead. Or me.

—Geraldine Page

☆ ☆ ☆ ☆

Natalie Schafer is famous as the actress who never acts with her hands below her elbows.

—Jim Backus

☆ ☆ ☆ ☆

When all that silly publicity was zooming in on Gina Lollobrigida's and Sophia Loren's boobs, I was looking at their waists. Perfect, tiny little waists! I was green with envy. You don't see little waists like that anymore.

—Natalie Wood

☆ ☆ ☆ ☆

Mae West did have an hourglass figure. She had, besides, a minute attention span.

—Cary Grant

☆ ☆ ☆ ☆

Randolph Scott was tall, blond, and handsome. Who cares if he was Cary Grant's better half or not? The point is, he stayed out in the sun too often, doing all those westerns. Then he turned into leather. Sunshine does that.

—Anne Baxter

☆ ☆ ☆ ☆

Have you seen Robert Redford lately? He looks like the proverbial sun worshipper who's changed into a lizard. That skin! And in close-up yet!

—Klaus Kinski

☆ ☆ ☆ ☆

Alec Baldwin is this big new alleged sex symbol. But he has eyes like a weasel! He makes Clint Eastwood look like a flirt.

—Sandy Dennis

☆ ☆ ☆ ☆

Somebody said Tom Selleck was a male model. That's more his calling. When he was younger, he was great-looking. It's when he walks and talks that he has problems. He's rather goofy for a macho sex symbol, and his voice is sort of high-pitched, and his laugh...never mind!

—Aldo Ray

☆ ☆ ☆ ☆

The least sexy actress I ever saw was that girl...yeah, the star of *That Girl*, Marlo Thomas. Like a kewpie doll with a bad hairdo and not even cute.

—Cornel Wilde

☆ ☆ ☆ ☆

I smoke a pipe. Is that so unusual? Women in Scandinavia have been smoking pipes for centuries. Why do people stare? If I were Marlene Dietrich smoking a cigar, I don't think they'd stare. Do you have to be European to be permitted an idiosyncrasy?

—Joan Hackett

☆ ☆ ☆ ☆

People tend to overlook feet. I've been complimented on mine. You don't see that many men's feet in American movies. Elvis had good-looking feet. You know who has really great-looking feet? This sounds like an inane topic...but Timothy Dalton, the new James bond. Check them out. They're the type of feet you'd want to have.

—James Franciscus

☆ ☆ ☆ ☆

Forrest Tucker, who was on *F Troop* on television, has a daily ritual at his country club. He falls asleep, or he pretends to be asleep, with only a towel over his middle, after he has taken a shower. Club members go into the locker room, they take their guests—I have personally seen this—and they quietly lift the towel. It is an awe-inspiring sight, because Mr. Tucker is more than well endowed!

They say that one of the guests who was brought in to view Mr. Tucker had just been traveling in Arizona but was more impressed by what he saw at the country club. He is supposed to have shouted, "Fuck the Grand Canyon!"

—Fernando Lamas

☆ ☆ ☆ ☆

I once asked Milton Berle how big he gets when it's fully erect, 'cause even at half-mast it's world-class. And he said, "I don't know—I always black out first."

—Sammy Davis Jr.

☆ ☆ ☆ ☆

A producer once said to my agent in front of me, "She looks too much like a cat." Then the producer laughed, looked at me, and asked my agent, "Does she act like one?" I told the producer, "No, and neither did Simone Simon in *The Cat People*." I felt like scratching his eyes out.

—Capucine

☆ ☆ ☆ ☆

It bothered me that my brother [Tom Conway] physically resembled me. Before he came out [to Hollywood], I asked that he not use my surname. He arrived in 1939, and anyone fleeing the war in Europe was not well viewed in England. Of the actors who left England for the States, they said they had "gone with the wind up." Tom took over the Falcon series when I'd tired of it, and I was amazed when he made a go of it—he had more luck with it than I did. But that was the acme of his career....His resemblance to me helped him at first; later, it was a handicap. Tom was a nice fellow; it's too bad for him he was my brother.

—George Sanders

☆ ☆ ☆ ☆

I'm a white American who went to France and became a movie star there. Blacks and whites went to Europe, and some of us hit the jackpot in France or Germany. Europe loves American gumshoe types, and I'm no beauty. George Nader came here when he was tossed out of Hollywood, and he did pretty good for himself. He'd have done even better if he'd been a little ugly, like me.

—Eddie Constantine

☆ ☆ ☆ ☆

Edith Piaf was one of the great loves of my lifetime. Tiny, tiny dame—"the sparrow." Huge, enormous personality and singing voice, a legend in France. But she wore herself out, wore herself to a frazzle through hard living and hard drinking. Drugs, too. The life force inside her was gargantuan, but it couldn't keep competing with her systematic destruction of her body. She didn't last half a century, and we who knew and loved her were surprised her body held out that long.

—Eddie Constantine

☆ ☆ ☆ ☆

Fat's cute on a kid. It's not cute on an adult, not a middle-aged one. It just hangs there....Lots of us ex-kiddie stars now hanging out over the belt: me, Shirley Temple, Jane Withers, the Our Gang crowd, lots of us. When you stop being a star, you lose your incentive.

—Jackie Coogan

☆ ☆ ☆ ☆

George Zucco had a demented look in the eyes, on and off the soundstage. Always playing mad scientists and evil doctors....It's rumored that he actually did go mad. I've never heard anything to prove it, but I know that as an actor, he gave even me the shivers!

—Boris Karloff

☆ ☆ ☆ ☆

Joel Grey and Roddy McDowall. I was disappointed to see that eventually even they couldn't conquer the aging process. Nobody's a boy forever, and there truly are no portraits of Dorian Gray....

—Frankie Howerd

☆ ☆ ☆ ☆

Aren't Sydney Greenstreet and John Houseman the same person?

—Humphrey Bogart

☆ ☆ ☆ ☆

One of his colleagues says Walter Brennan doesn't really limp. It's a stunt he does, for career purposes. You know, anything for the old image!

—Chill Wills

☆ ☆ ☆ ☆

I always thought Jane Fonda had a stunning figure. Did you see *Barbarella*? Why did she need to go and have her breasts enlarged? Just 'cause Tom Hayden had an affair with a younger woman? That was a real letdown to me. What kind of role model seeks to solve her private problems or boost her career by making her bust bigger?

—Sandy Dennis

☆ ☆ ☆ ☆

Lotte Lenya had a boob job at eighty. Even when she was young, she had the face of a frog. Loaded with personality, but a frog-face! And lifting her bosom at eighty! That's hope taken to an insane degree.

—Nancy Walker

Wasn't Dom DeLuise fat enough? Most fat people don't know when to quit. They go from chubby to fat...and at fifty it is disgusting, and then they go to extra fat and then monstrous. I would shoot myself before letting myself get so fat! Your land of plenty is becoming a land of fat people.

—Marcello Mastroianni

☆ ☆ ☆ ☆

That singer, Billy Idol, has the sneeringest, meanest-looking lower lip I've ever seen. It's sexy but stupid. Is he just doing a bad Elvis pout, or was he born that way?

—Freddie Mercury

☆ ☆ ☆ ☆

The French may be a sensuous people, but their actors are ugly! The latest is Gérard Depar-doo [Depardieu]. That is a sex symbol? To who, lady truck drivers? And they had Yves Montand, who looked like a Gallic frog, and Jean-Paul Belmondo, with the squashed nose. What, don't they have any handsome actors there?

—Halston

☆ ☆ ☆ ☆

Too thin is too thin, especially when you get older and all the veins show. Audrey Hepburn thin was lovely as a girl, but now she looks pained, with that scrawny chicken neck, and I do love her....Mia Farrow nowadays just looks bedraggled. The same with Diana Ross—she looks like she just arrived from Ethiopia.

—Judith Anderson

☆ ☆ ☆ ☆

The ugliest actor I have ever seen? William Hurt—no, *John* Hurt, the English one. I mix them up. William Hurt is plain, but John Hurt is downright ugly. Even his voice.

—Yul Brynner

☆ ☆ ☆ ☆

Rex Harrison used to joke that he was sometimes mistaken for Chinese because of his eyes. Ah, but always a mandarin or some very upper-caste Chinese, he'd insist to me, as though it mattered. Rex has a terrifically high opinion of himself.

—Richard Burton

☆ ☆ ☆ ☆

Elvis Presley wound up looking on the outside like what he always was on the inside—an overrated slob.

—Joan Blondell

☆ ☆ ☆ ☆

Goldie Hawn has a great body, and she's kept it. But she has the face of a chicken, and that plus her giggle is what kept her from being sexy or a sex symbol.

—Andy Warhol

☆ ☆ ☆ ☆

Kathryn Grayson not only kept her lovely figure, she's added so much to it....

—Bob Fosse

☆ ☆ ☆ ☆

I like Whoopi Goldberg. It's her hair that scares me.

—Don Rickles

☆ ☆ ☆ ☆

Poor Roseanne whatever-her-name-is-now. She manages to lose twenty or thirty pounds, but who can tell?

—Don Rickles

☆ ☆ ☆ ☆

Joan Crawford was notorious for her falsies. Even lying down, she wanted to have an upright bosom for the screen. The older she got, the more concerned she was with keeping it up. It got rather pathetic, because it became her main worry in most of her scenes. That, and her wigs and falls. I was there, I witnessed it. It was gruesome.

—Diana Dors

Marty Feldman's eyes did for his career what Dolly Parton's boobs do for hers—not that much. At first you look, out of curiosity; then you think of the person as belonging to those bulging eyes or the huge knockers. It's a drawback, although I'd like to have seen them costar, because Marty's eyes would always look as if he'd just seen Dolly's boobs for the very first time!

—Graham Chapman of *Monty Python*

☆ ☆ ☆ ☆

David Bowie has one blue eye and one brown eye. Two colors, which makes sense—he has two faces.

—Graham Chapman

☆ ☆ ☆ ☆

The tie for the biggest shoulders in Hollywood history has to be between Joan Crawford and Anthony Perkins. Both of them psychos!

—Joan Hackett

☆ ☆ ☆ ☆

It's too bad they don't have voice-lifts. Jimmy Stewart's voice was barely tolerable when he was young. Now it's a trial to listen to. Fortunately, he never has anything interesting to say.

—Judith Anderson

☆ ☆ ☆ ☆

That myth about big noses don't hold true. Otherwise, Jimmy Durante would have been the biggest lover in Hollywood. I heard he was about average and not unusually active. Now, Chaplin was short and his nose was average, but his pecker was really big-time, and he was forever prowling after young girls to keep it warm for him!

—Mae West

☆ ☆ ☆ ☆

Where Jayne Mansfield went wrong was entering the movie business. With melons like that, she should have entered the circus. If she'd been serious about acting, she could have had them reduced. I hear Loni Anderson did, and she's not exactly what I'd call a serious actress.

—Aldo Ray

☆ ☆ ☆ ☆

You know Bette Midler? Big talent but a face like a lemon. Have you seen her husband? He makes her look almost beautiful. These star broads don't marry for love; they marry for contrast.

—Sam Kinison

☆ ☆ ☆ ☆

Talk about the decline and fall of the Roman Empire! It's almost as shocking as the decline and fall of Jack Nicholson's face.

—Ugo Tognazzi

☆ ☆ ☆ ☆

Brooke Shields, or as I call her, Dress Shields. Just a model, though a model of what, I don't know. She's too tall to be a leading lady and too short to act.

—Geraldine Page

☆ ☆ ☆ ☆

Now Michael Jackson says his skin turned white by itself. What about his nose, his lips, and his hair? Did they also decide to turn Caucasian by themselves?

—Boy George

☆ ☆ ☆ ☆

Why is it today's actors look like male hookers? Alec Baldwin, Richard Grieco, Kiefer Sutherland.... They look like they haven't slept for days—except maybe for money. And the other actors—James Woods, Gary Oldman, Stallone—they look like they're pimps. How did Tinseltown get so ugly?

—Anthony Perkins

☆ ☆ ☆ ☆

The names have gotten out of hand. Rock Hudson or Tab Hunter, that was bad enough. The first names were asinine, but the guys were handsome and sexy. How can you take seriously guys who aren't handsome, aren't talented, and have names like River Phoenix and Keanu Reeves?

—Klaus Kinski

☆ ☆ ☆ ☆

Beautiful women are not funny. Can you feature Grace Kelly as a comedienne?

—Phyllis Diller

☆ ☆ ☆ ☆

Phyllis Diller used to be hilarious. Then she had all those face-lifts, so now she looks good...and she's dull.

—Leonard Bernstein

☆ ☆ ☆ ☆

Tom Cruise is plastic. He's cute, all right, but it's surface. That's not even his real name. It's all a façade, but beautifully packaged, so he's a star.

—Johnnie Ray

☆ ☆ ☆ ☆

I always admired Katharine Hepburn's cheekbones. More than her films. She always wanted to be liked. Too much so. But I'd have killed for those cheekbones!

—Bette Davis

☆ ☆ ☆ ☆

What's the opposite of an aphrodisiac? To me, it's Woody Allen. He's a sex maniac, at least on the screen. But he has sex appeal-minus.

—Curt Jurgens

☆ ☆ ☆ ☆

All these stereotypes about Jewish actresses! We don't all look like Streisand or Midler. Some of us are Lauren Bacall or Dinah Shore or Jill St. John or *me*! Or even that Marilyn Monroe type on *Gilligan's Island* [Tina Louise as Ginger Grant].

—Sylvia Sidney

The proof that looks are only half of the stellar equation is Isabella Rossellini. She looks just like her mother [Ingrid Bergman] did at that age. But she lacks the class, the personality, the magic. A clone is but a clone....

—Joan Hickson (Miss Marple)

☆ ☆ ☆ ☆

Melanie Griffith is a child actress. Still. She couldn't play smart to save her life. Additionally, she makes movies with [husband] Don Johnson. Being a dumb blond must run in that family.

—director Derek Jarman

☆ ☆ ☆ ☆

The least sexy actor in America? Let me think....John Malkovich. From head to toe and including the name, he is completely unappetizing and unbelievable. I'm sorry, John.

—Gilda Radner

☆ ☆ ☆ ☆

I was out walking the other day. Passed Ray Walston. From *My Favorite Martian*. Nice guy. He loves nature in spite of what it did to him.

—Forrest Tucker

☆ ☆ ☆ ☆

Dick Cavett thinks he's TV's brightest, funniest star. What ever gave him that idea? He's far from the funniest, just the shortest.

—Bette Davis

☆ ☆ ☆ ☆

Merv Griffin talks almost as much as his guest. Talk show hosts should get it through their heads that the *interesting* one is the guest, not the host. The host is just a singer or actor who couldn't make it. Or got too fat.

—Rudy Vallee

☆ ☆ ☆ ☆

Ed McMahon. What a concept. Talk about a sow's ear....Rich, famous, and absolutely useless.

—Sam Kinison

☆ ☆ ☆ ☆

Alec Baldwin is too mean looking to be a sex symbol. That is my feeling. For me, a sex symbol should offer the hope of a good time. He looks like he would beat you up if you said one word wrong!

—Ursula Andress

☆ ☆ ☆ ☆

Rob Lowe really is. I used to think his talent lay in his face, but apparently it is much lower than that....

—Klaus Kinski

☆ ☆ ☆ ☆

Albert Finney was a big talent. Now he's just big.

—George Rose

☆ ☆ ☆ ☆

Kathleen Turner certainly has a weight problem. Also dark roots, a floundering career, and Burt Reynolds keeps bad-mouthing her in interviews. And she's not getting any younger. When can we expect to see her doing dinner theater, I wonder?

—Frankie Howerd

☆ ☆ ☆ ☆

Those two boy wonders from *Beverly Hills 90210* [Jason Priestley and Luke Perry]...they look like they share one brain. And four penises. There's nothing there but lots of aimless, overrated testosterone.

—Derek Jarman

☆ ☆ ☆ ☆

Jeanne Moreau was interesting-looking—to put it nicely. Now she looks like Bette Davis, and that is not putting it nicely.

—Van Johnson

Boris Karloff was a good actor because he was a kindly man and in no way scary. Bela Lugosi was not a good actor because he was not a pleasant man and he was plenty scary, as is!

—Sal Mineo

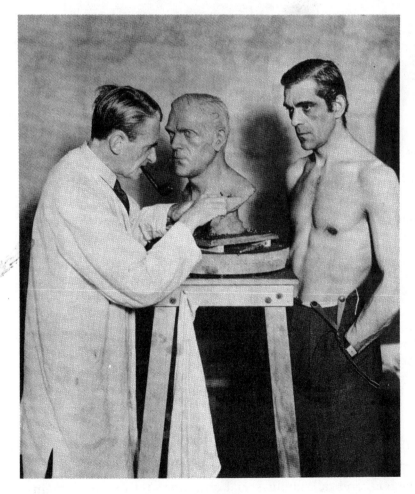

Boris's bust: sculptor and Karloff

Latin lover Lupe Velez and longtime lover Gary Cooper

Gary Cooper has the longest dick in town, but no ass to push it with.

—Lupe Velez

☆ ☆ ☆ ☆

I respect and admire Estelle Winwood; after all, she's so old, you almost have to. I think it's so quaint that she's making a whole new career out of merely being very old. But I hope *I* never live so long that I get hired simply for not being a corpse!

—Elsa Lanchester

☆ ☆ ☆ ☆

What is this thing that blondes get from the press? Special immunity by way of hair color? Look at Grace Kelly. She couldn't act, she was arrogant, anti-Semitic, snobbish, and alcoholic, and talk about social climbing! Yet the press maintained this image of her as some perfect princess. Why? Because she was a beautiful blonde? We all knew that Aristotle Onassis, who owned the Monte Carlo casino, ordered Prince Rainier to marry a Hollywood blonde for the publicity and tourism.

It was rumored that Rainier almost chose Marilyn Monroe. If he had, no doubt she, too, would have been immortalized by the media as virginal, talented, and a nonaddict....At least Marilyn wasn't a hypocrite. Unlike Grace, she didn't pretend to be a sanctimonious virgin.

—Anne Baxter

Cow Eyes: Estelle Winwood

You can always tell the gay actors. They're the ones who have the plain or ugly wives. Or live with an ugly girl. Look at Tyrone Power or Rock Hudson, to mention two I can legally name. Or that famous TV star or that homely male singer. Besides, most of the gays in Hollywood are good-looking. They don't let themselves go to pot or fat, like Chevy Chase or Dan Aykroyd. Gay actors prize their looks, and so do their easily fooled public!

—Anne Baxter

☆ ☆ ☆ ☆

The prettiest actress?...Probably Vivien Leigh. The least? Martha Raye. Miss Raye had great legs...but such a mouth. I could say something nasty, but I'm too much of a gentleman. Besides, I'm allergic to lawyers and fish.

—Cecil Beaton

☆ ☆ ☆ ☆

I tell you, some of those Golden Age character actresses, you could have attached a feedbag to them and it wouldn't have looked out of place. Edna May Oliver. Or Flora Robson. Or Charlotte Greenwood. Great gals, talented, too, but real horse-faces!

—George Cukor

☆ ☆ ☆ ☆

I think the handsomest actor in pictures was Gilbert Roland. If he hadn't been from Mexico, he could have been up there with Gable. He had the sexiest bedroom eyes, a killer smile, he was drenched in 'It.' He married Constance Bennett, and although she denied it, she was irked by the fact that when they went out together, even though she was the bigger star, he became the center of attention due to his great looks. I love those Latin looks!

—Lucille Ball

☆ ☆ ☆ ☆

Mae West walked like a female impersonator. Nor was her bust as large as its reputation. She made mountains out of mo-

lehills.... She wasn't inherently beautiful, but her sexual personality and suggestiveness supplied everything she didn't have.
—David Janssen

☆ ☆ ☆ ☆

Alfred Hitchcock was like a eunuch. For one thing, he was a voyeur. Terrified of sex but dying to watch or peep. He was fat and squishy and the most asexual man I've ever known.
—James Mason

☆ ☆ ☆ ☆

John Travolta looks like a combination of Rudolph Valentino, with that vaselined hair, Kirk Douglas, with that dimple in his chin, and a street hustler.
—Gérard Depardieu

☆ ☆ ☆ ☆

My nomination for the ugliest actor today would be Sonny Bono, except he can't act. Neither can Cher, but at least she's easy on the eyes.
—Cornel Wilde (Cher later won an Oscar for Best Actress)

☆ ☆ ☆ ☆

I'd have to say the homeliest actress in our business was Margaret Hamilton. She played the Wicked Witch of the West, and they painted her green, but she really didn't need any makeup. And she was a dear, lovely lady. As opposed to those gorgeous actresses who were usually impossible bitches!
—Robert Preston

☆ ☆ ☆ ☆

Charles Laughton was fat. He was fat when he was young, and he told me that his one solace was that he at least would never lose his looks to age, as he had none to lose. The real tragedy is when great beauty gives way, and inevitably, what old age does to it— kills it, on a living face.
—Ingrid Bergman

John Goodman isn't fat. He's in a category beyond fat. What does one call it? Whalelike?

—Sam Kinison

☆ ☆ ☆ ☆

Roseanne Barr is smart. She's no Twiggy, so she gets this guy [Goodman] to play her husband, and next to him, she looks just pudgy.

—James Franciscus

☆ ☆ ☆ ☆

I saw this movie [*Jack the Bear*] with Danny DeVito in it. That mean little short chap from *Taxi*. In this, he had an awful wig or toupee on, and I swear, he looked like a demented munchkin! Didn't he ever look in the mirror while this movie was being made?

—Derek Jarman

☆ ☆ ☆ ☆

Dudley Moore has a club foot. That's not a problem—for him, his career, or anyone. What I object to is his club wit. Have you ever been chatted up by him at a cocktail party? Clichés abound....

—James Mason

☆ ☆ ☆ ☆

Fat tends to make people more androgynous and less individualistic. It's true! Fatty Arbuckle in drag looked just like a female, not like a male in drag....Or put a paper bag over the husband and wife on *Roseanne* and then see if you can tell which one is which gender....

—Ralph Bellamy

☆ ☆ ☆ ☆

Keith Richards looks like death warmed over.

—Joe Piscopo

Peter O'Toole looks like he's walking around just to save funeral expenses.

—John Huston

☆ ☆ ☆ ☆

James Coco looks like a bowling ball with legs. A *beige* bowling ball.

—Paul Lynde

☆ ☆ ☆ ☆

You may not believe this, but long ago, with a tan, and when he didn't distort his facial features with that sarcastic grin or waggle his head, Paul Lynde was actually good-looking.

—Allen Ludden

☆ ☆ ☆ ☆

Alice Ghostley [*Designing Women*] looks like a female Paul Lynde.

—Eve Arden

☆ ☆ ☆ ☆

Karl Malden's nose is an important sight in Hollywood. But I am curious: Was he born that way? What happened? He is too nice to ask him, but I am curious....

—Lila Kedrova

☆ ☆ ☆ ☆

Shelley Duvall has Bette Davis Eyes, but David Brenner has Barbra Streisand Nose.

—Wayland Flowers

☆ ☆ ☆ ☆

George C. Scott has Barbra Streisand's nose—or she has his.

—Gilda Radner

It's a sad thing. In later years, Fanny Brice had a nose job. She thought it would enhance her career. It didn't. She just wound up being less Fanny Brice....It was Dorothy Parker who said that Fanny cut off her nose to spite her race.

—Eve Arden

☆ ☆ ☆ ☆

[Michael Jackson] cut off his nose to spite his race.

—Marvin Gaye

☆ ☆ ☆ ☆

There's two kinds of exhibitionists that do nudity. The kind with a social conscience, like Richard Gere. And the kind without any conscience, or even talent, like Marky Mark. Then there's these anti-exhibitionist guys like Mel Gibson that bare their assets but not their family jewels, and put down the guys like Gere who've got more guts and maybe more up front....

—Ray Sharkey

☆ ☆ ☆ ☆

Cesar Romero isn't that far from ninety [born 1907]. I'm older, but he's the best-looking among Hollywood actors still alive. I imagine it's thanks to all that gay, carefree living. He's like Dorian Gray—with or without the second *r*.

—Judith Anderson

☆ ☆ ☆ ☆

Boris Karloff was born Henry William Pratt. All his friends call him Billy, and he is a pussycat. By nature, he should be playing kindly men, saintly men. Unfortunately, he has a horrifying face and a beastly Russian name and a spooky English accent, so he always plays murderers. Like me, but taller and scarier!

—Peter Lorre

☆ ☆ ☆ ☆

Garbo's face is stunningly beautiful. But it is a mask. It is a popular and prestigious product created by the moving picture business. But it bears little relation to the real woman behind the mask.

—Charlie Chaplin

Hail, Cesar Romero

Garbo (portrait by Sue Kutosh)

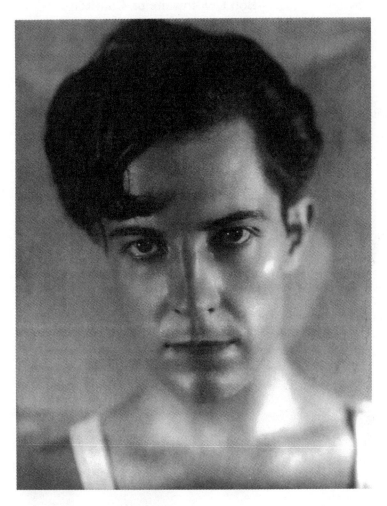

"Ravishing Ramón" Novarro

Ramón Novarro was one of the handsomest men in the movies. A big star. A beautiful star. But, like John Gilbert, who was heterosexual, Novarro didn't have the requisite deep voice. When those two men tried to speak in talkies, they came off as shriekies, and Gilbert's voice was even higher than Novarro's....It's a Hollywood double standard, because they've never penalized actresses with deep voices. Knowing Hollywood, it probably suspected Novarro and Gilbert of being lesbians!

—George Jessel

A toupée-wearing hack has-been.
> —Bob Goldthwaite on Charlton Heston

☆ ☆ ☆ ☆

Grace Jones came by in her macho outfit with a big raving beauty Swedish guy, like 6'6". Hans (later Dolph) Lundgren. And we shook hands and it was strange because he had such a weak handshake, really wimpy.
> —Andy Warhol

☆ ☆ ☆ ☆

Daniel Day-Lewis has what every actor in Hollywood wants. Talent. And what every British actor wants. Looks.
> —John Gielgud

☆ ☆ ☆ ☆

Fabio is the latest craze in America. He is an icon to the women who read romance novels there, but I think that the only big bosoms in which he is interested are his own!
> —Marcello Mastroianni

Index